Adult Coloring Book

Mandalas For Adults

Over 65 Exciting Designs

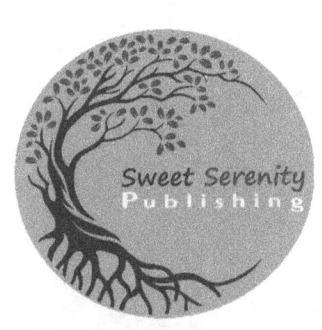

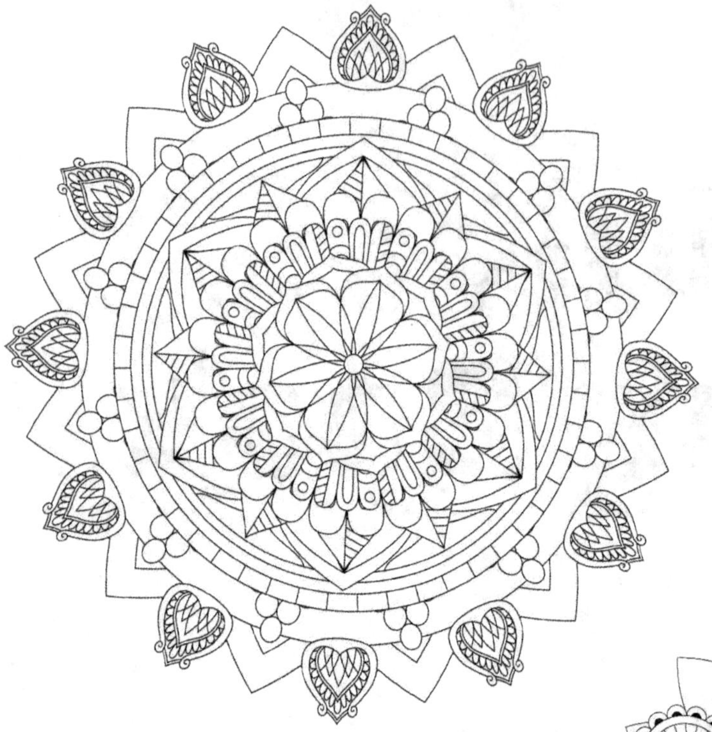

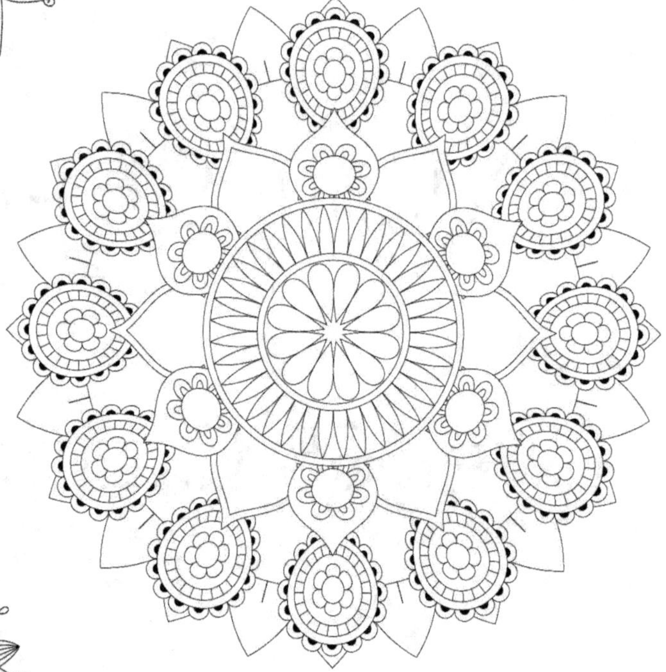

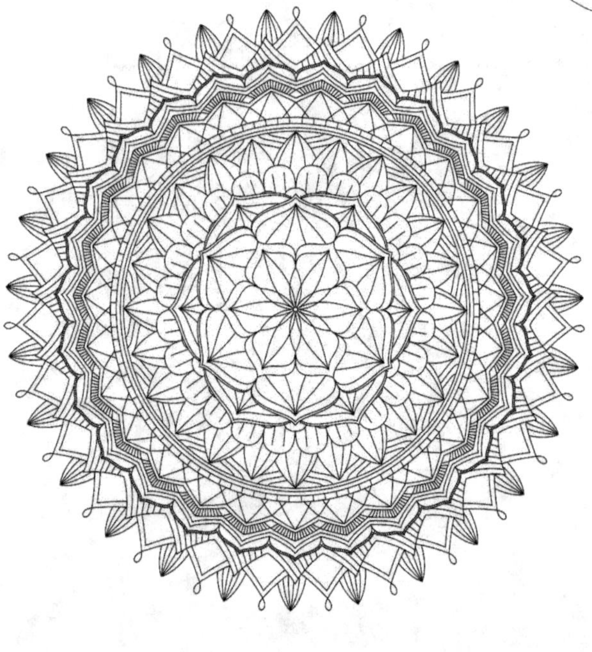

Copyright © 2020 Sweet Serenity Publishing

Contact -- sweetserenitypublishing@gmail.com

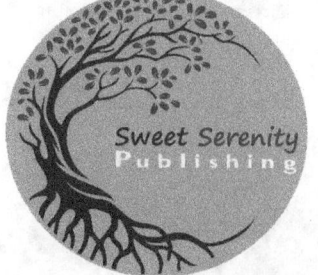

Our ultimate aim at Sweet Serenity Publishing is to bring you a little serenity – should you need it.

We design our products with your satisfaction in mind, and hope you enjoy this adult colouring book.

As well as the sixty-five main Mandala images that make up this book, we have included a small bonus section of twelve vintage images which were hand drawn on paper and turned into digital images.

We hope they bring you some pleasure.

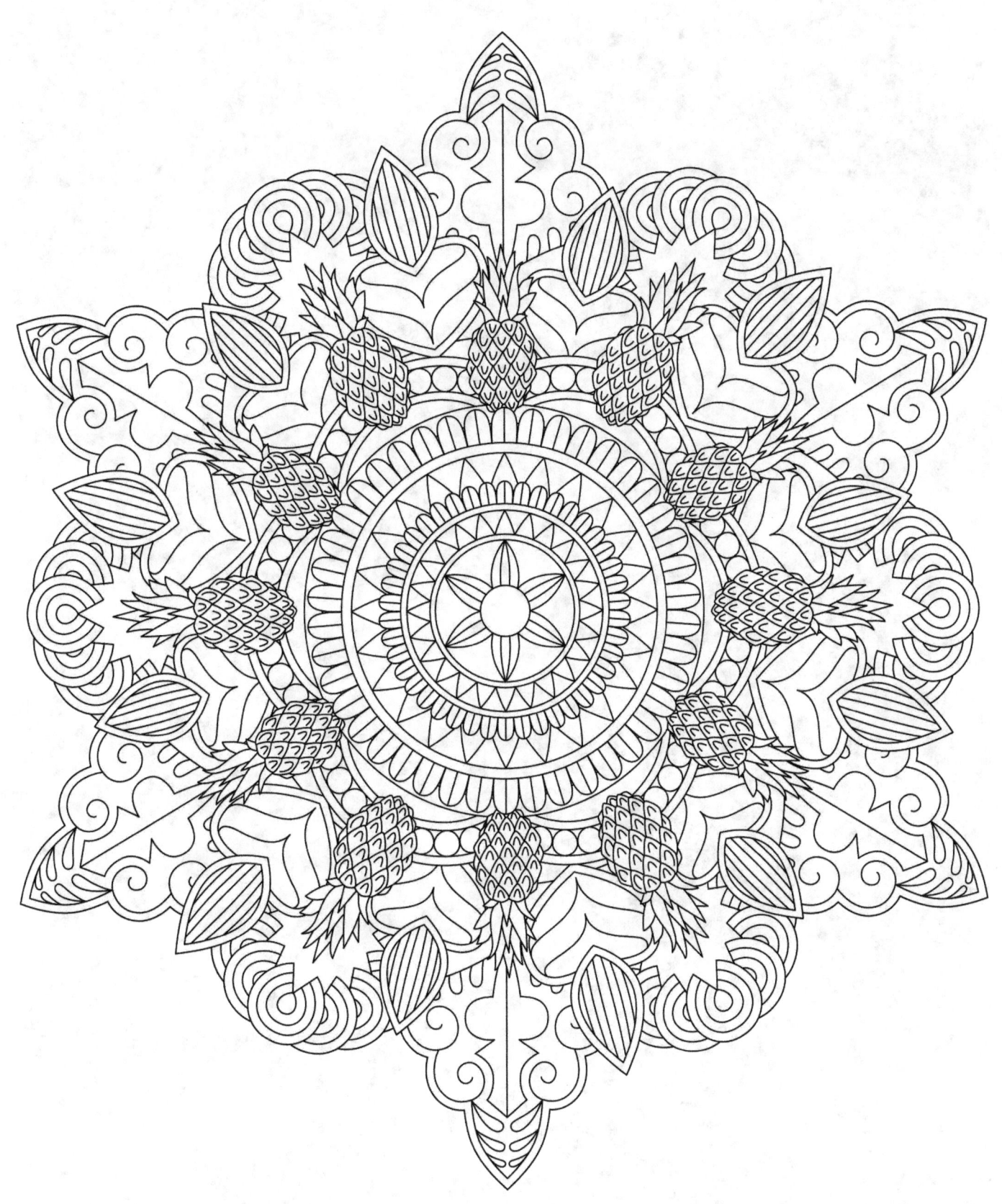

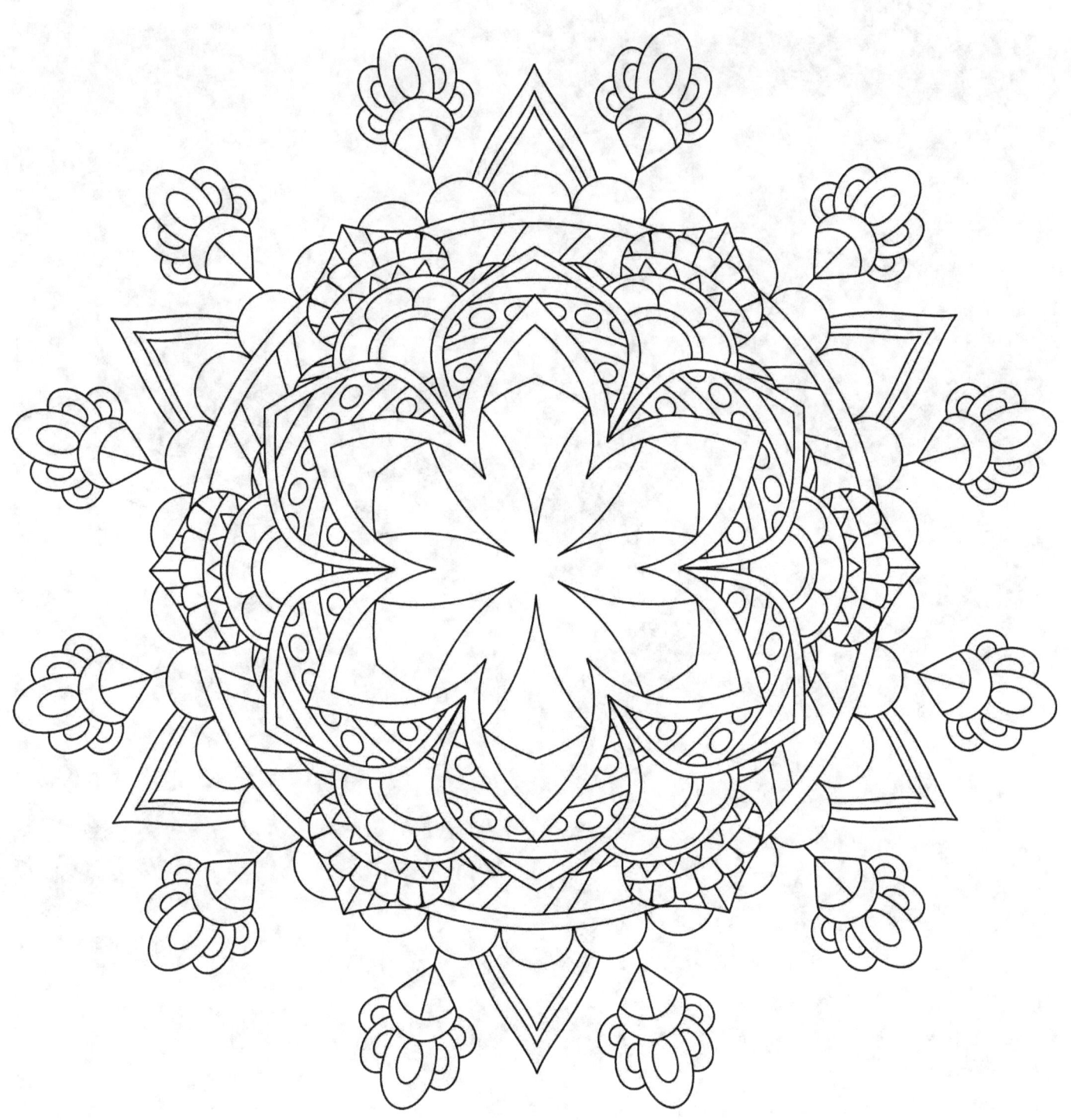

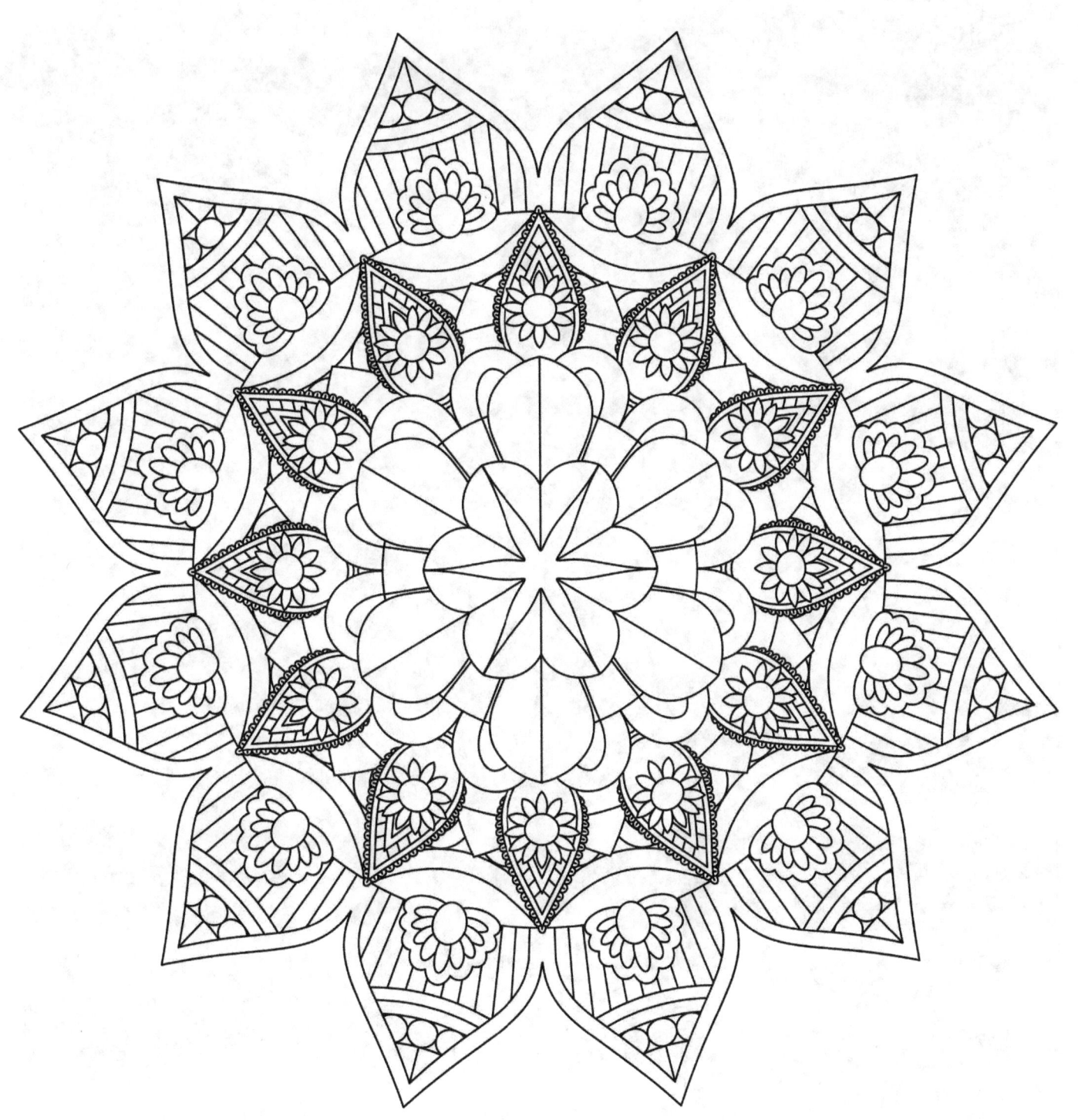

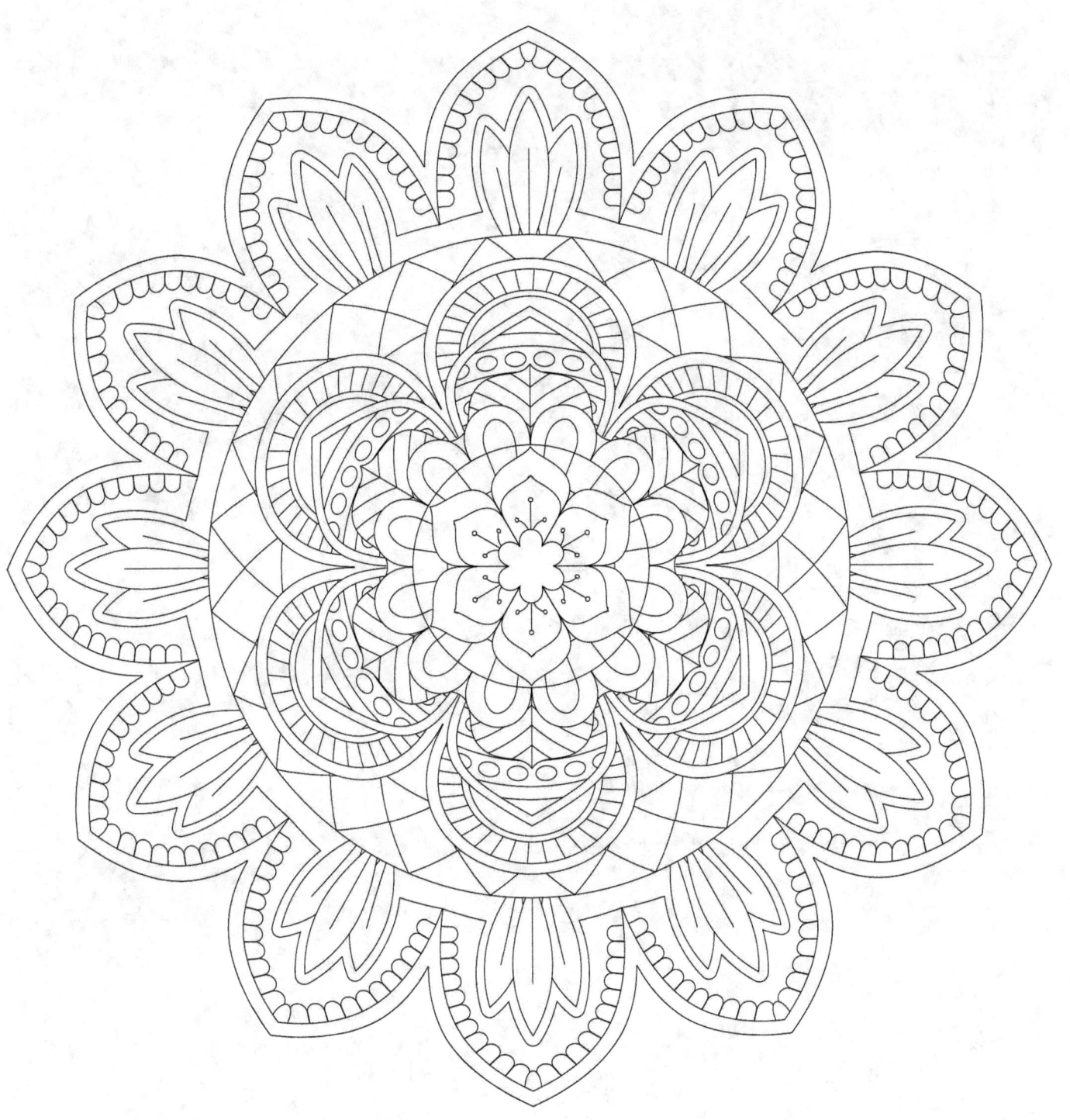

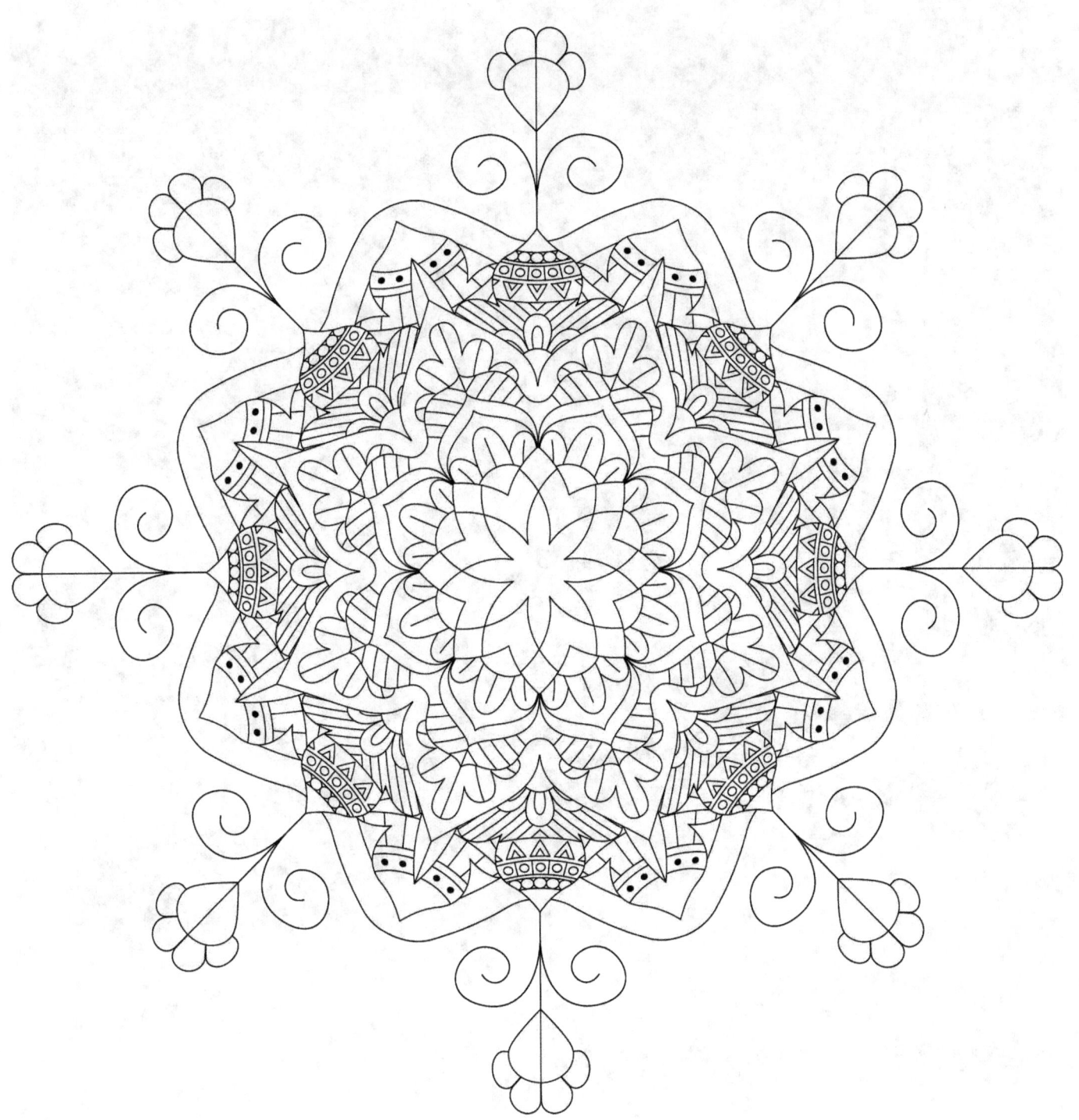

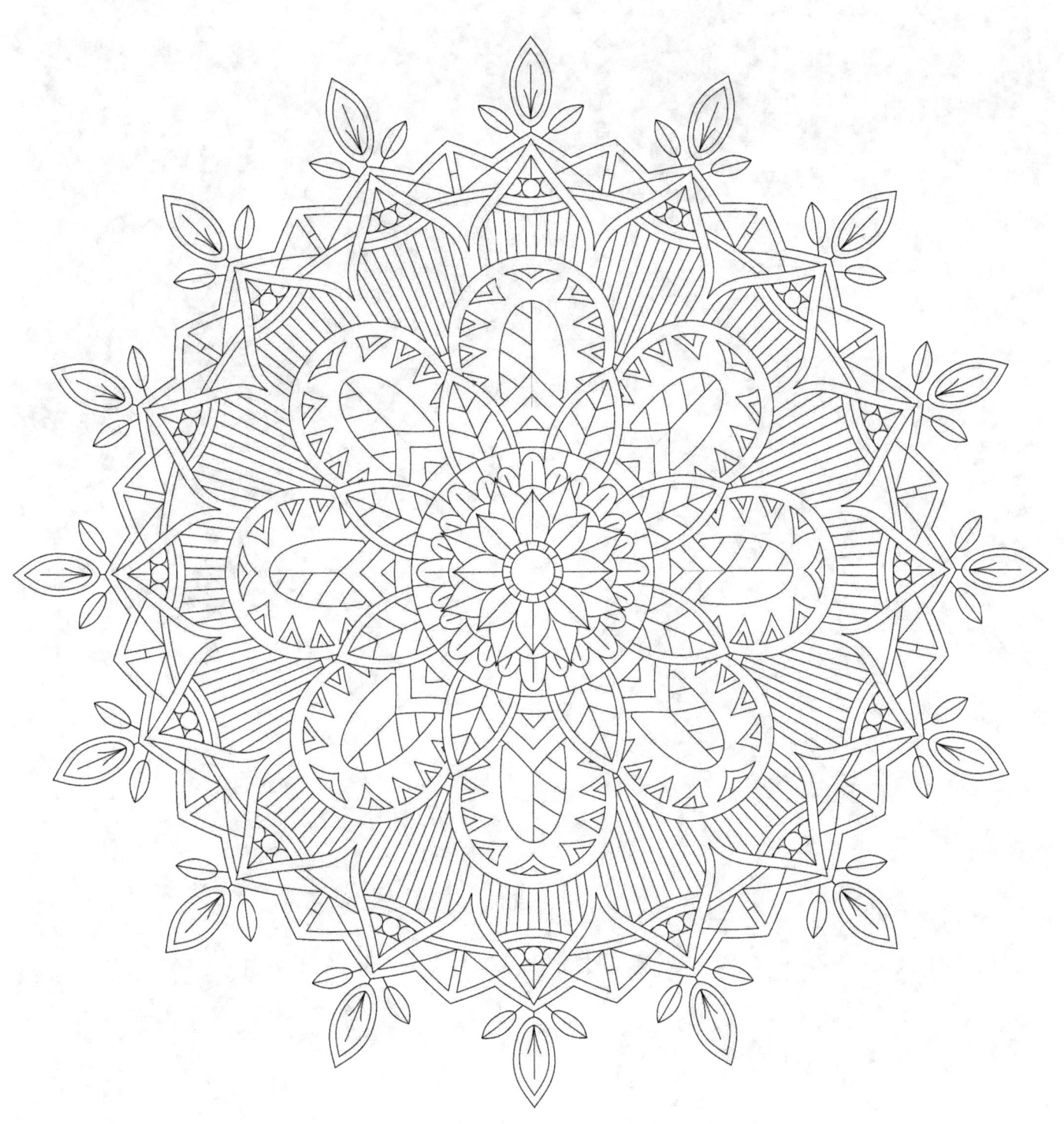

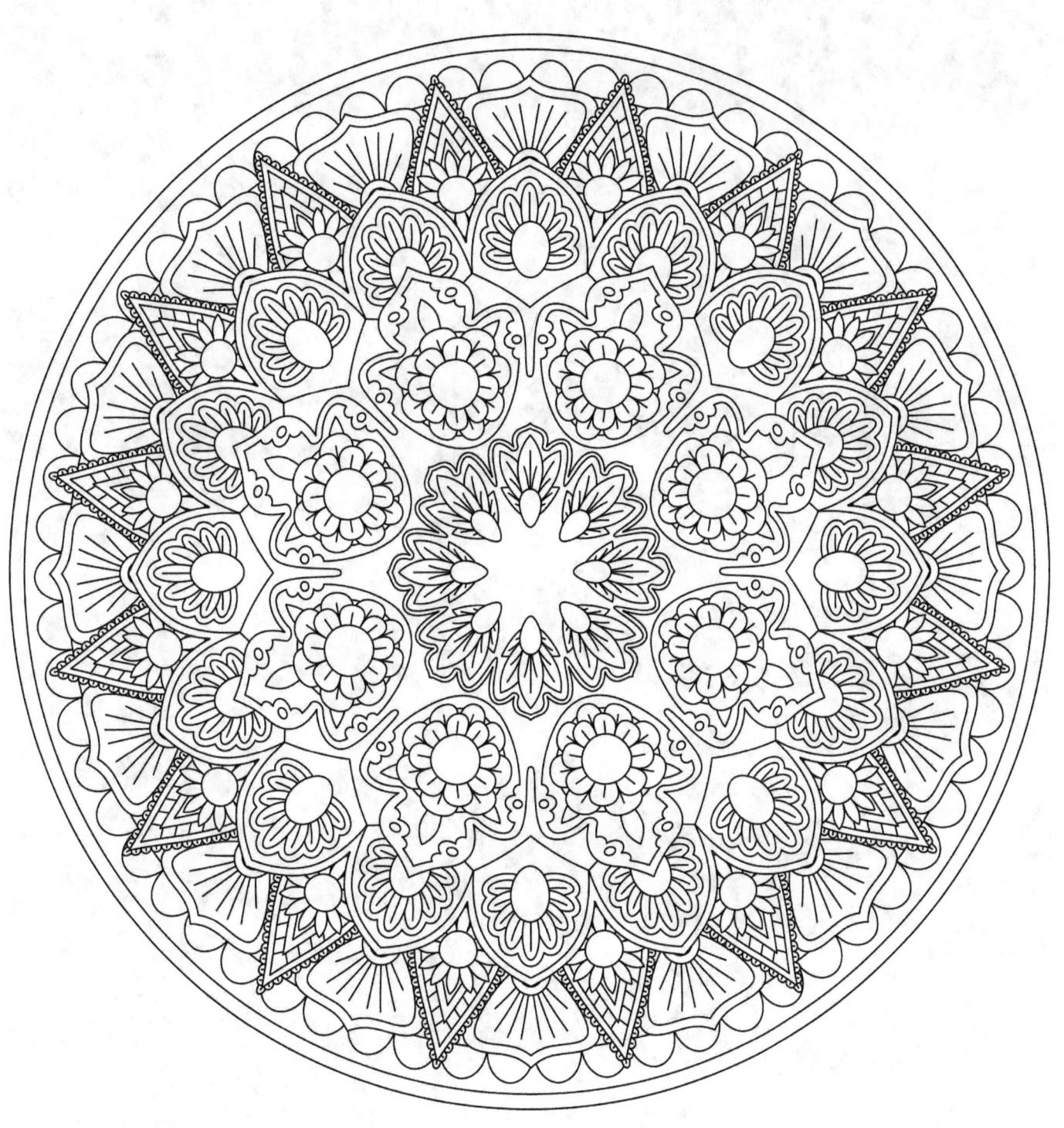

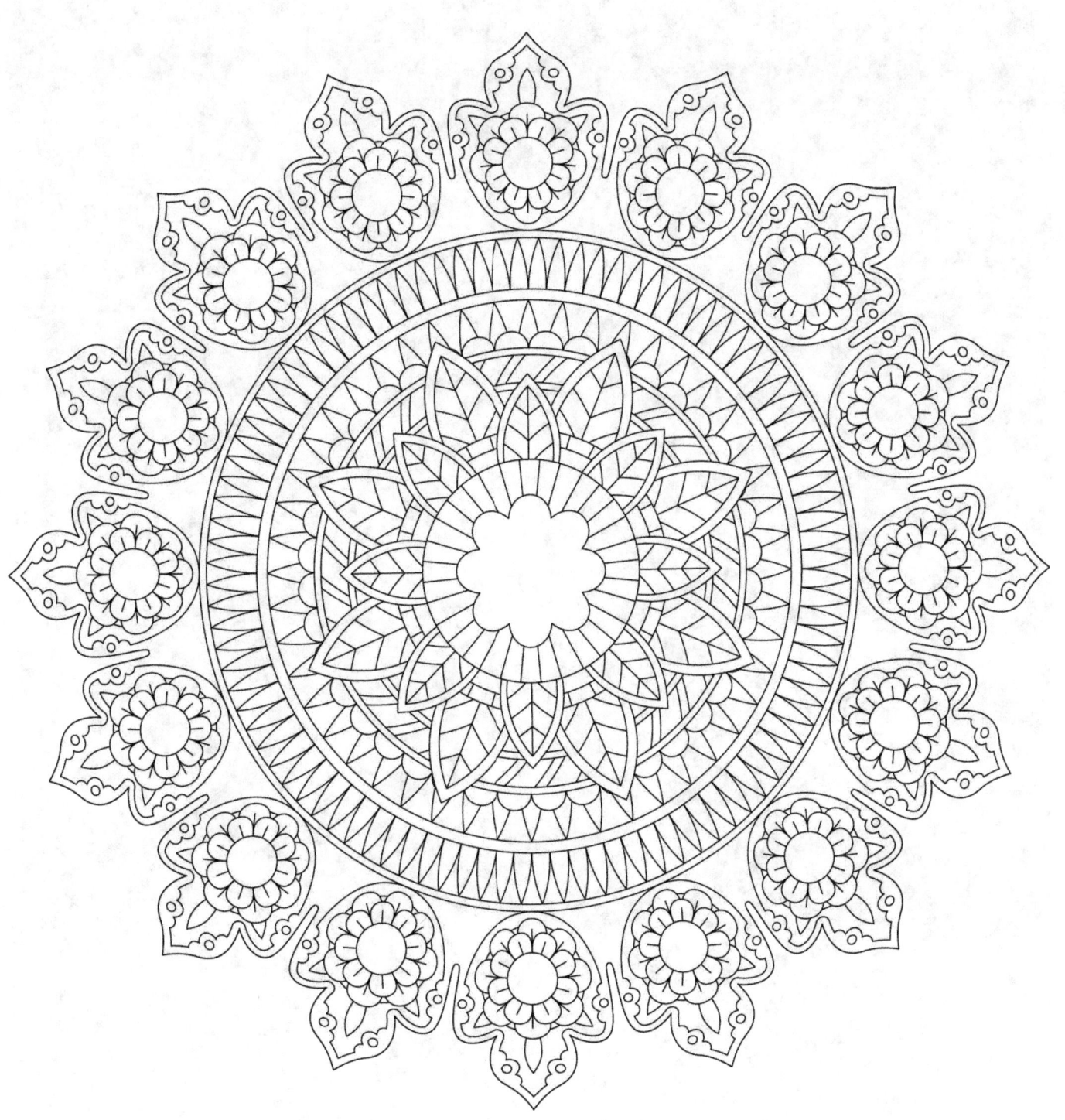

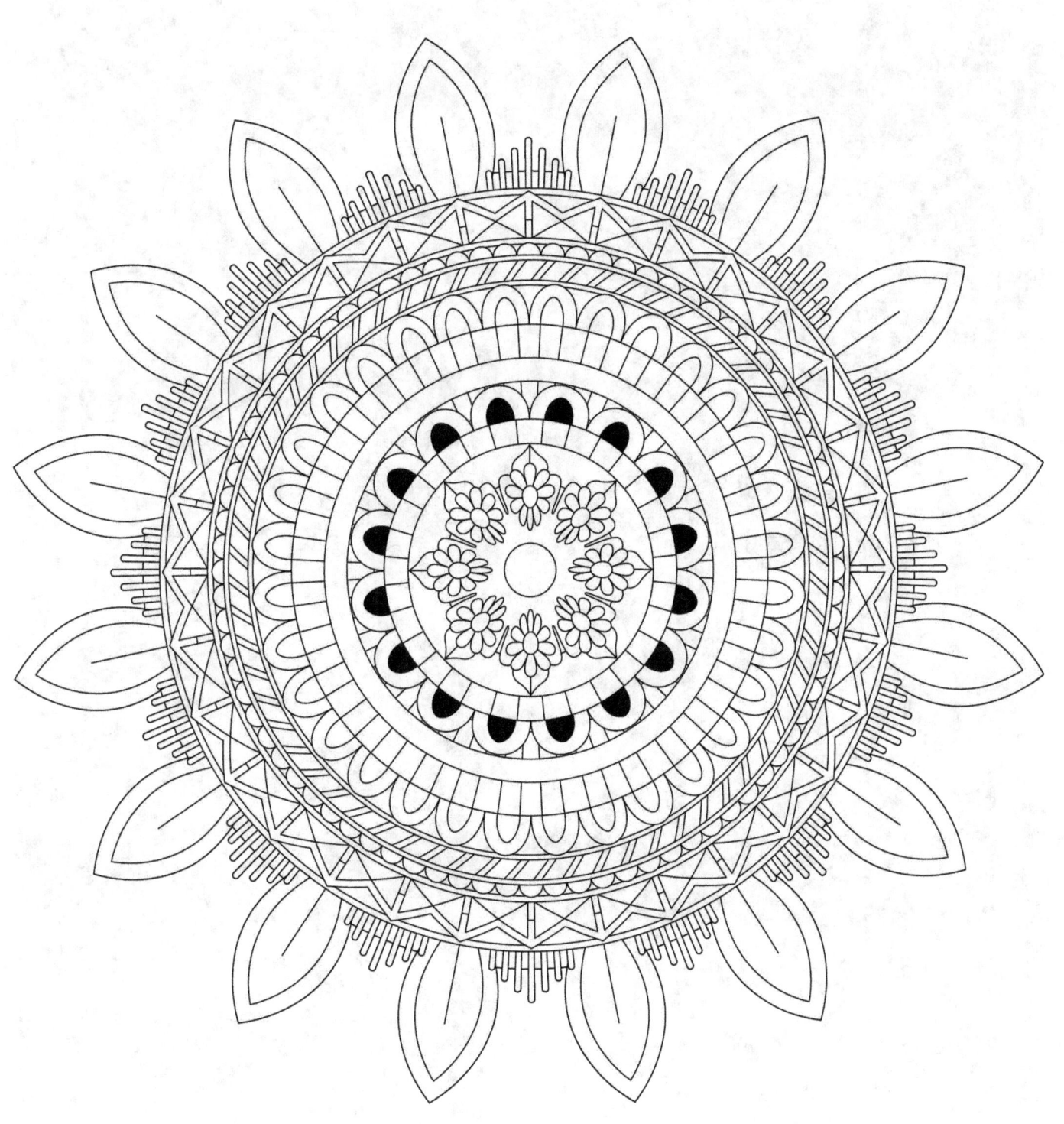

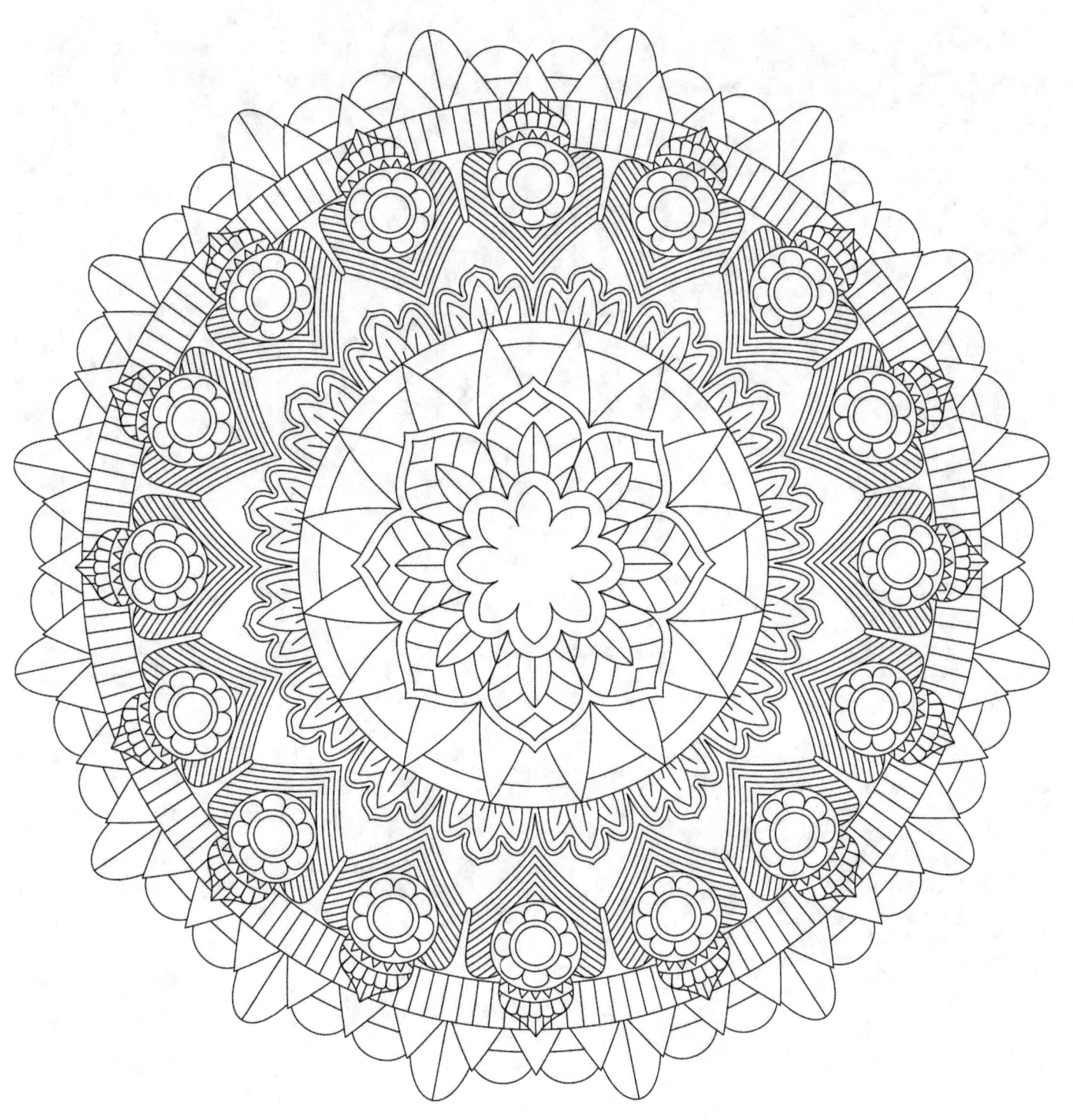

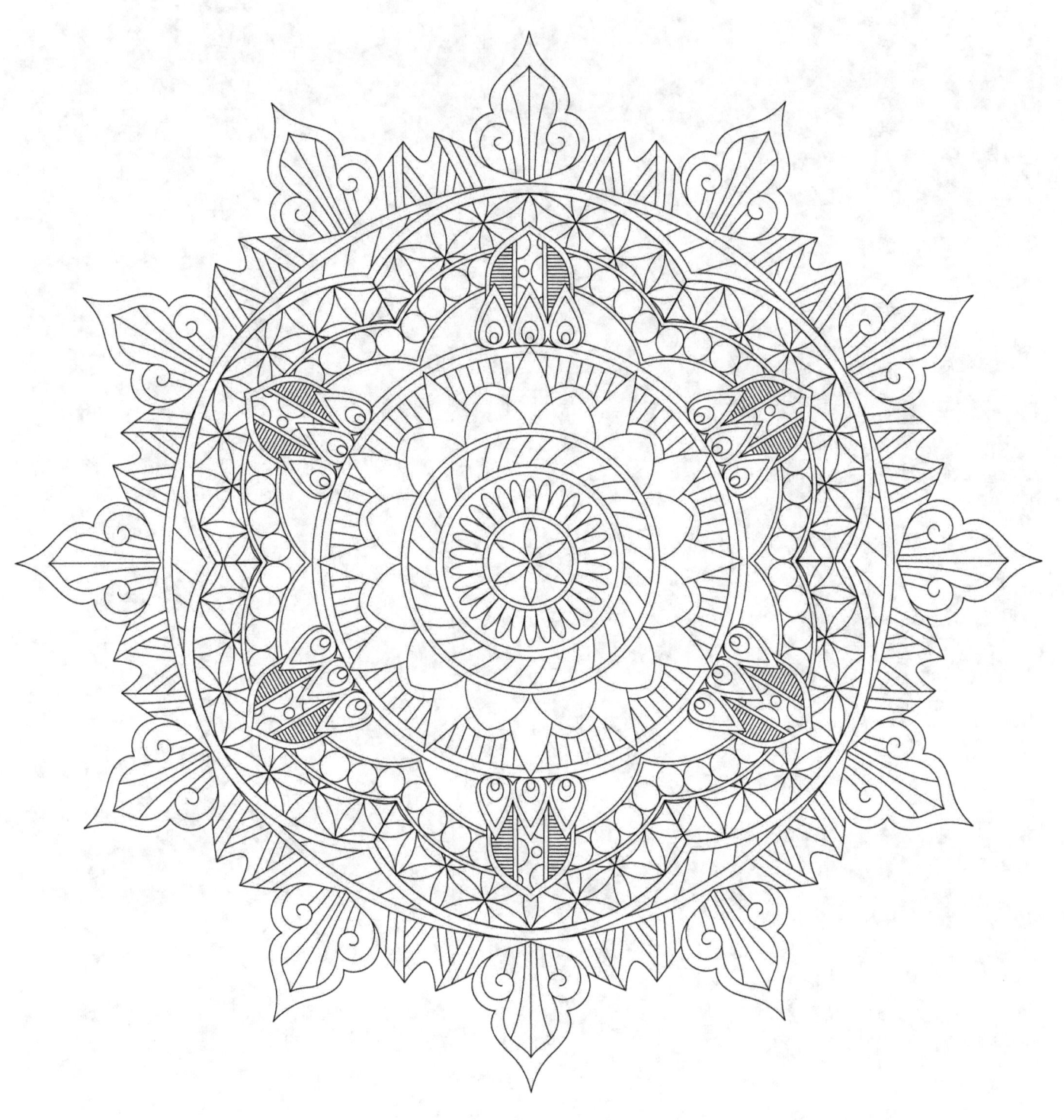

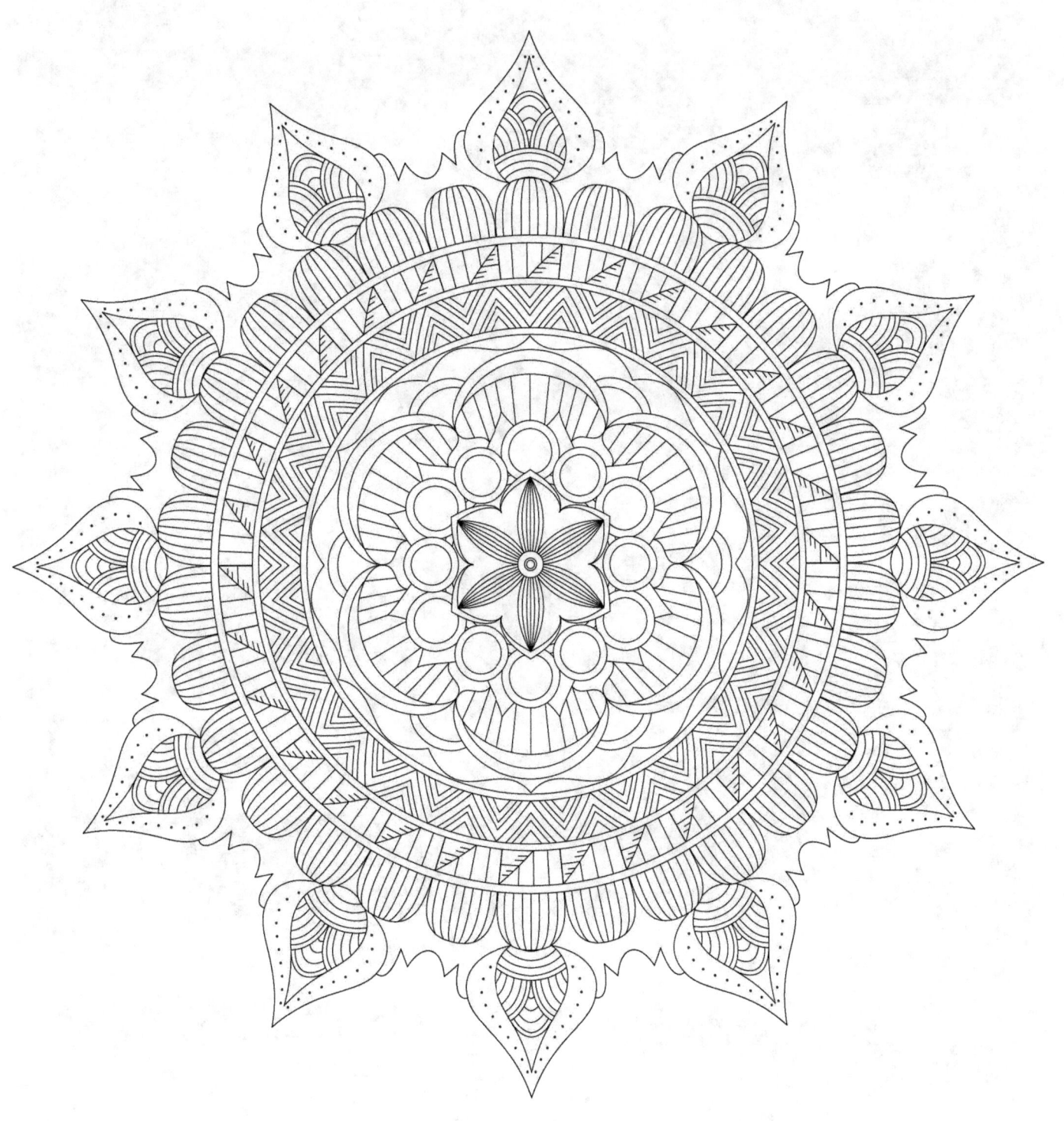

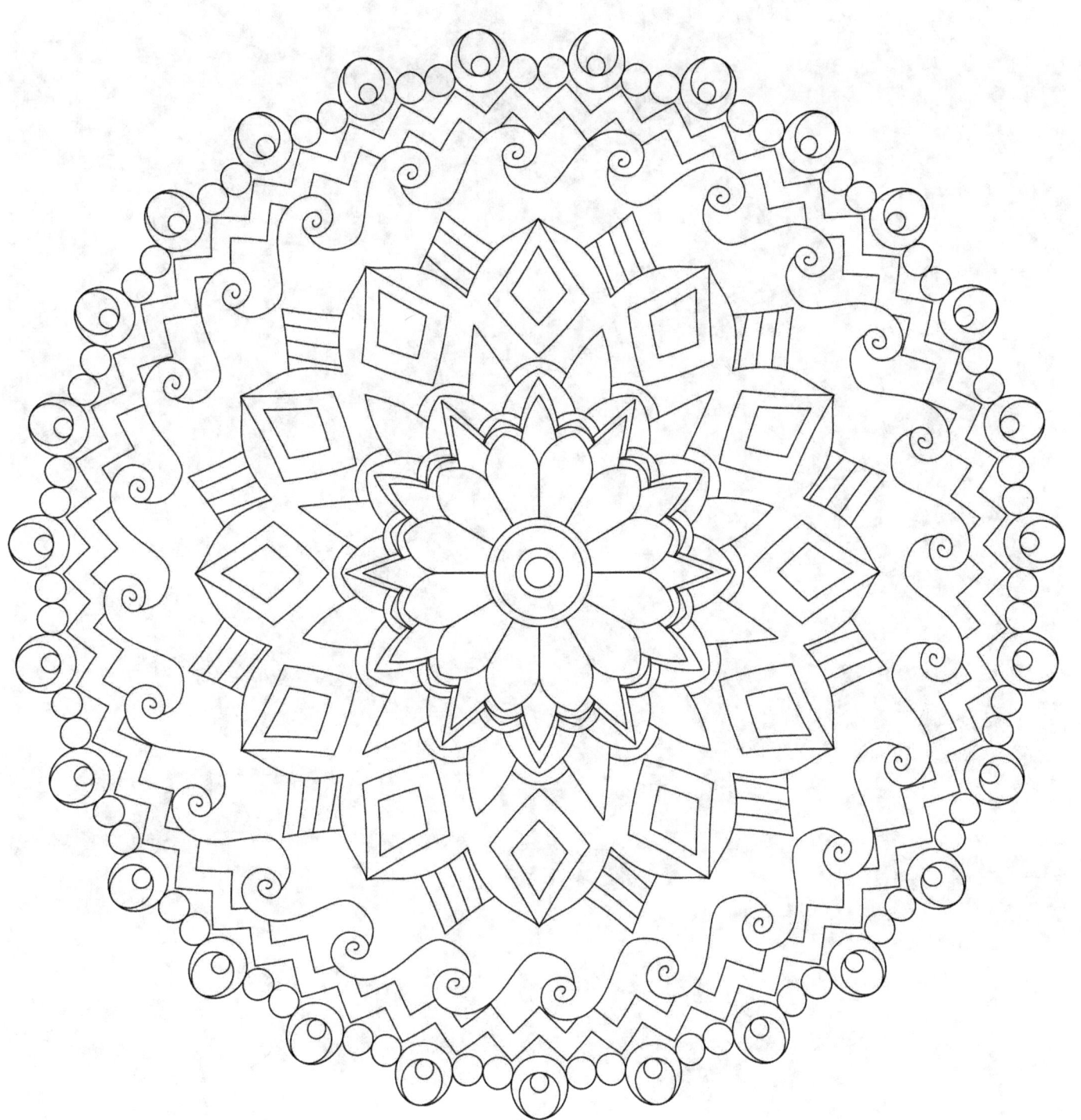

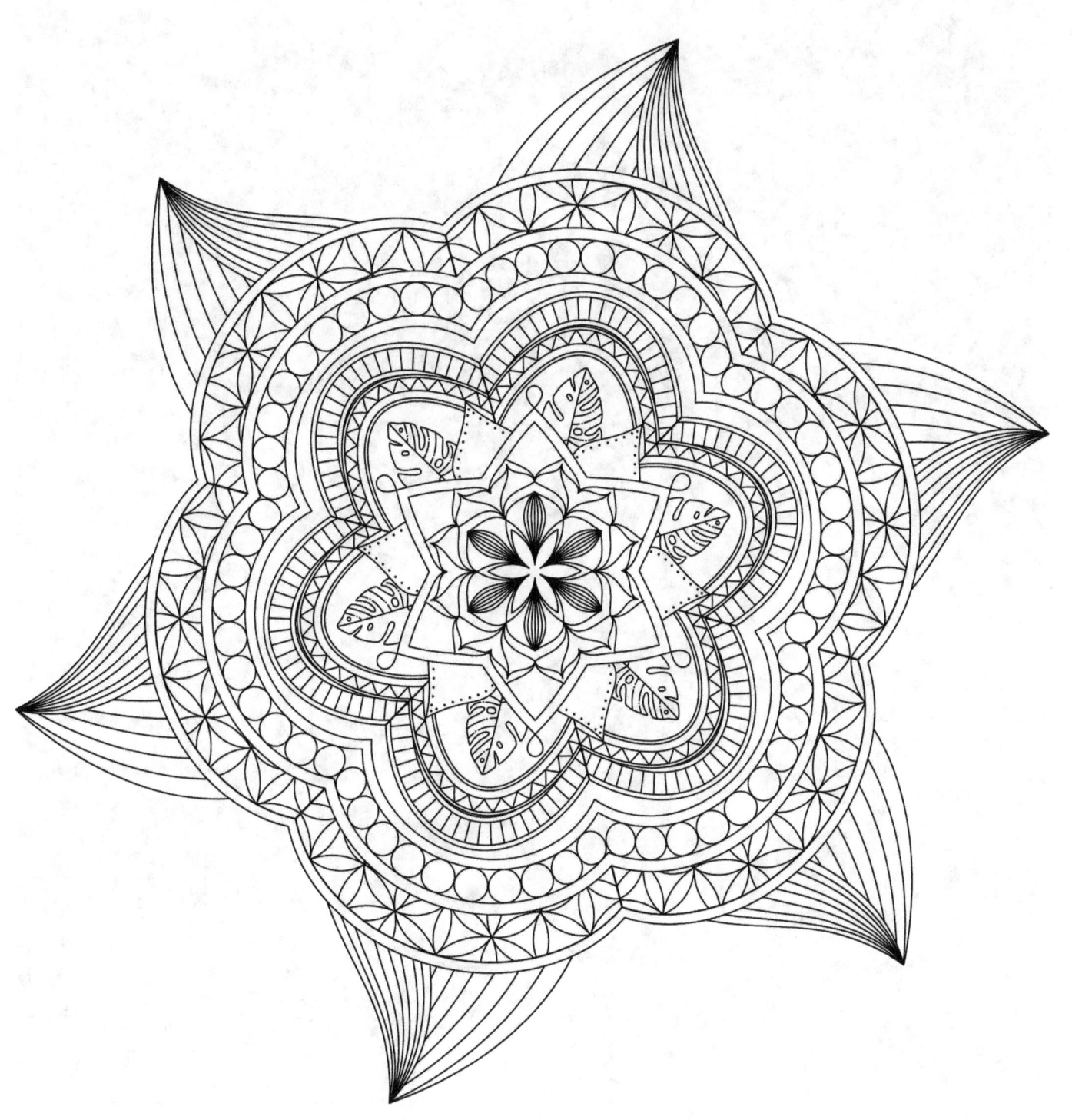

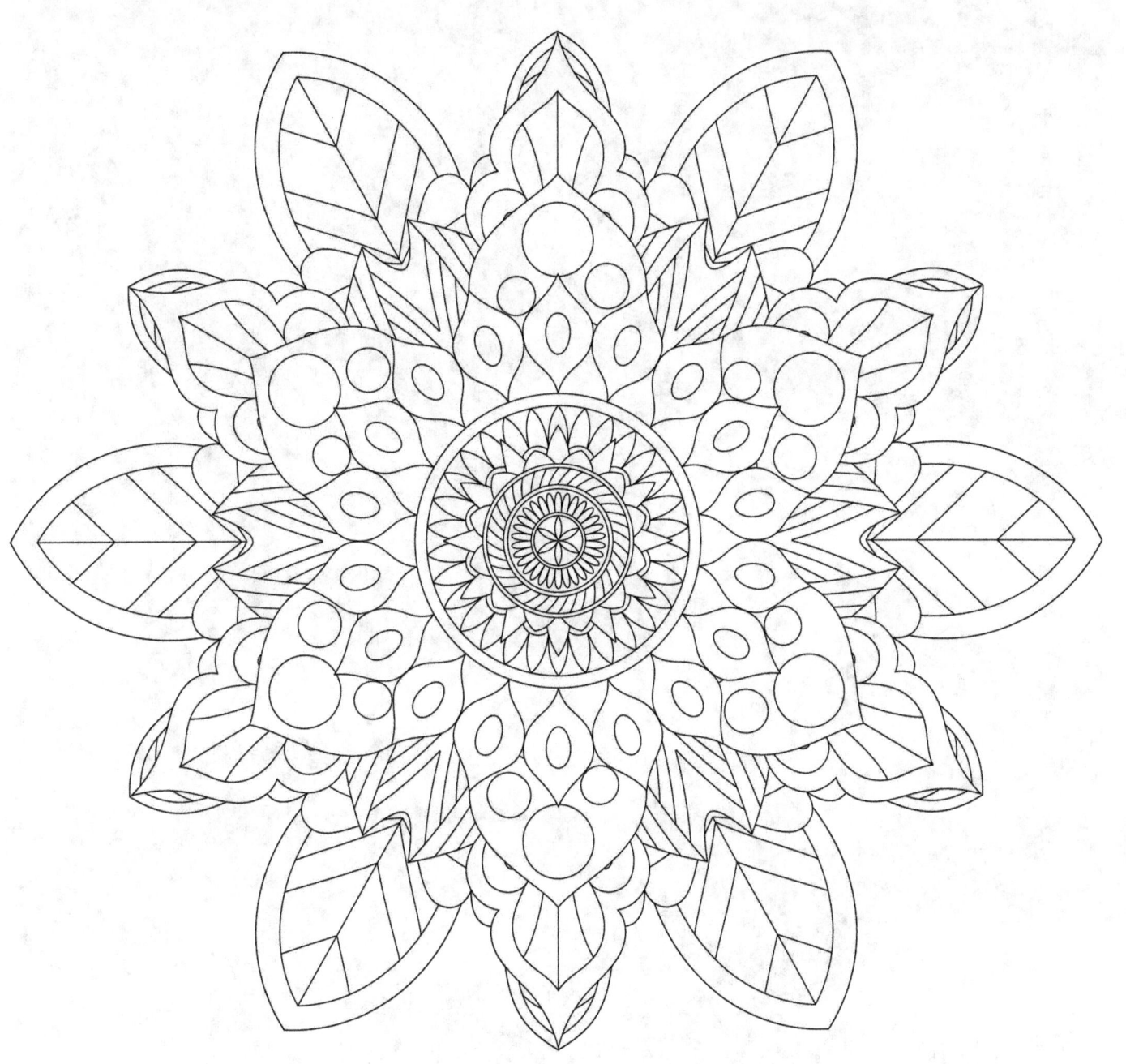

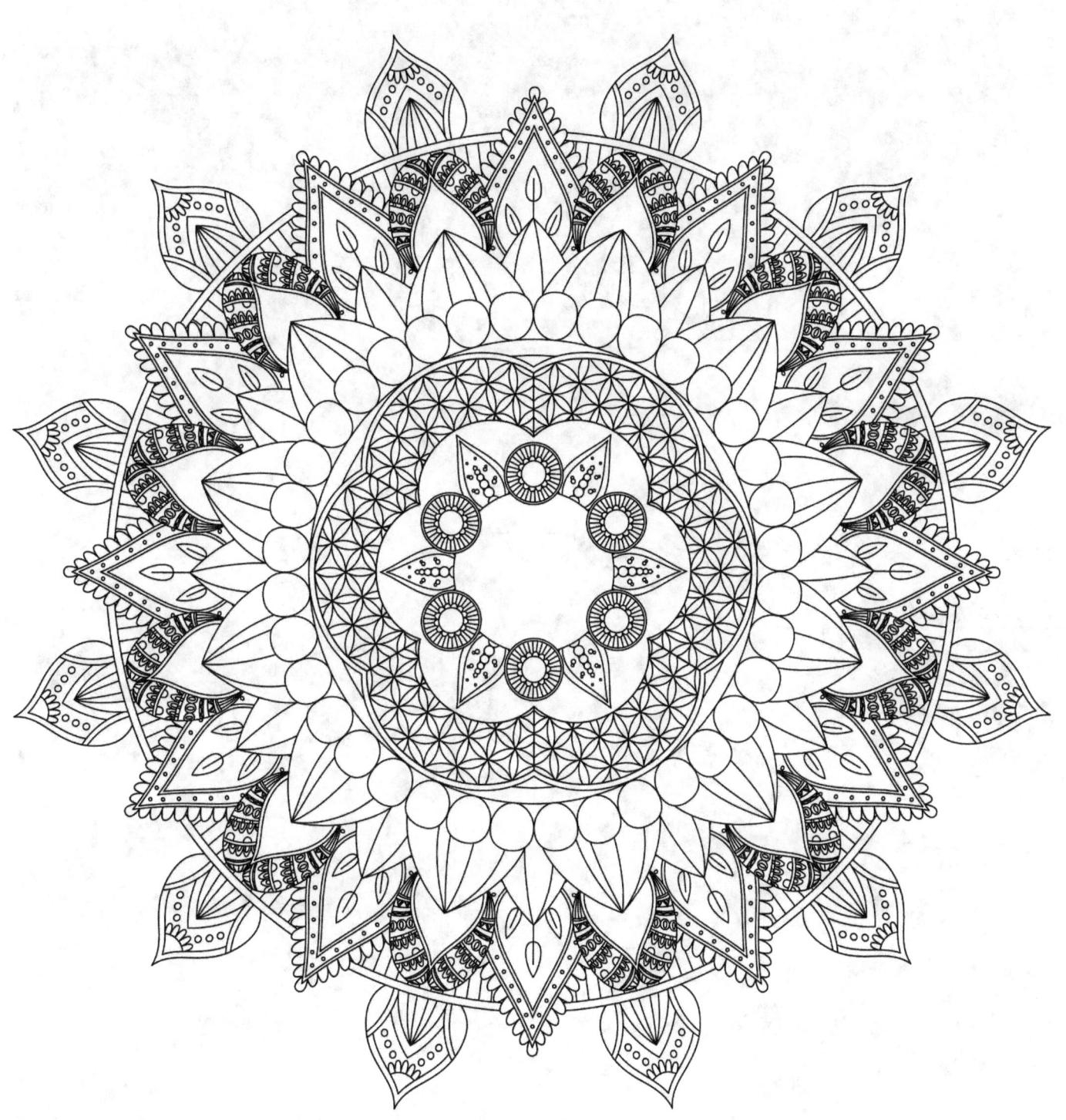

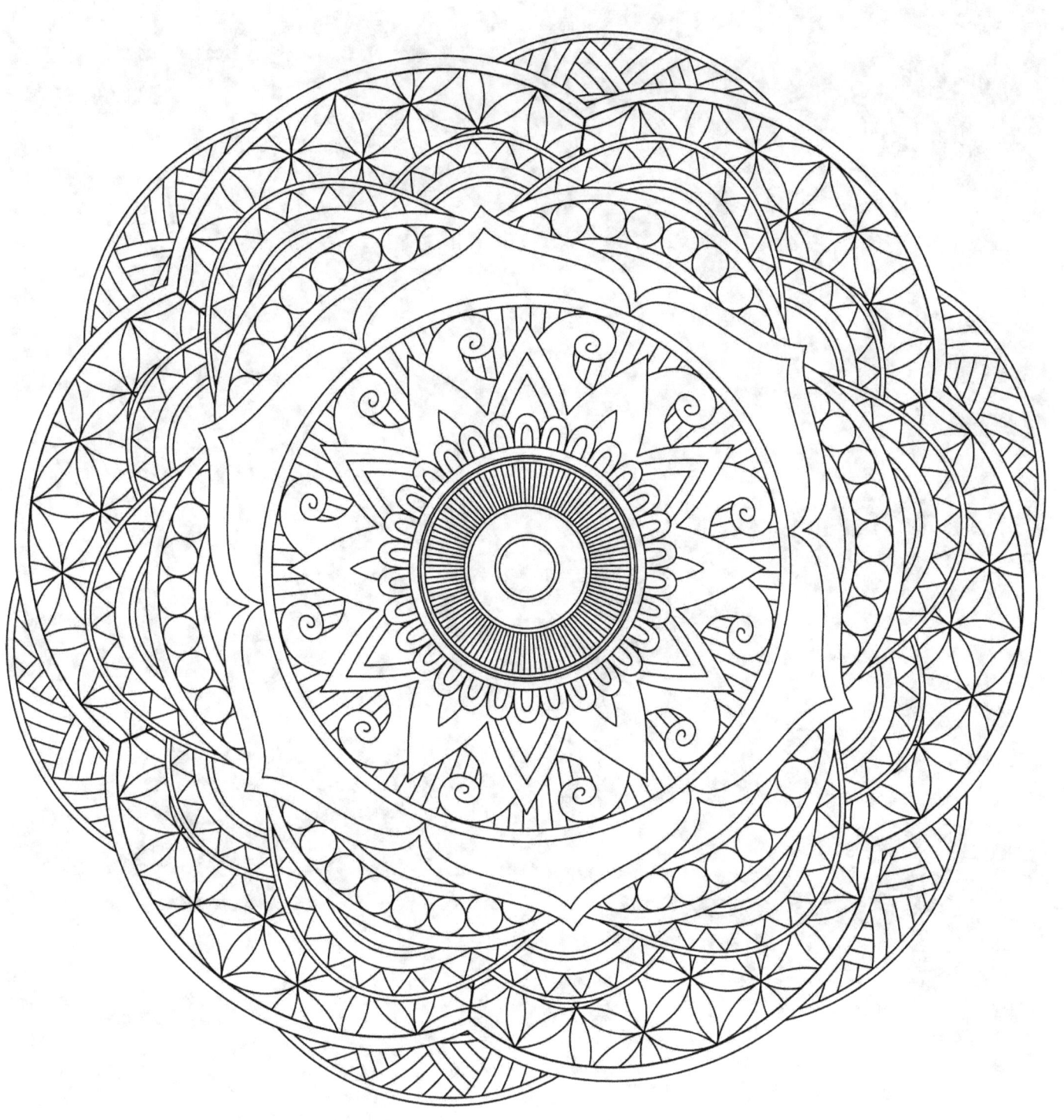

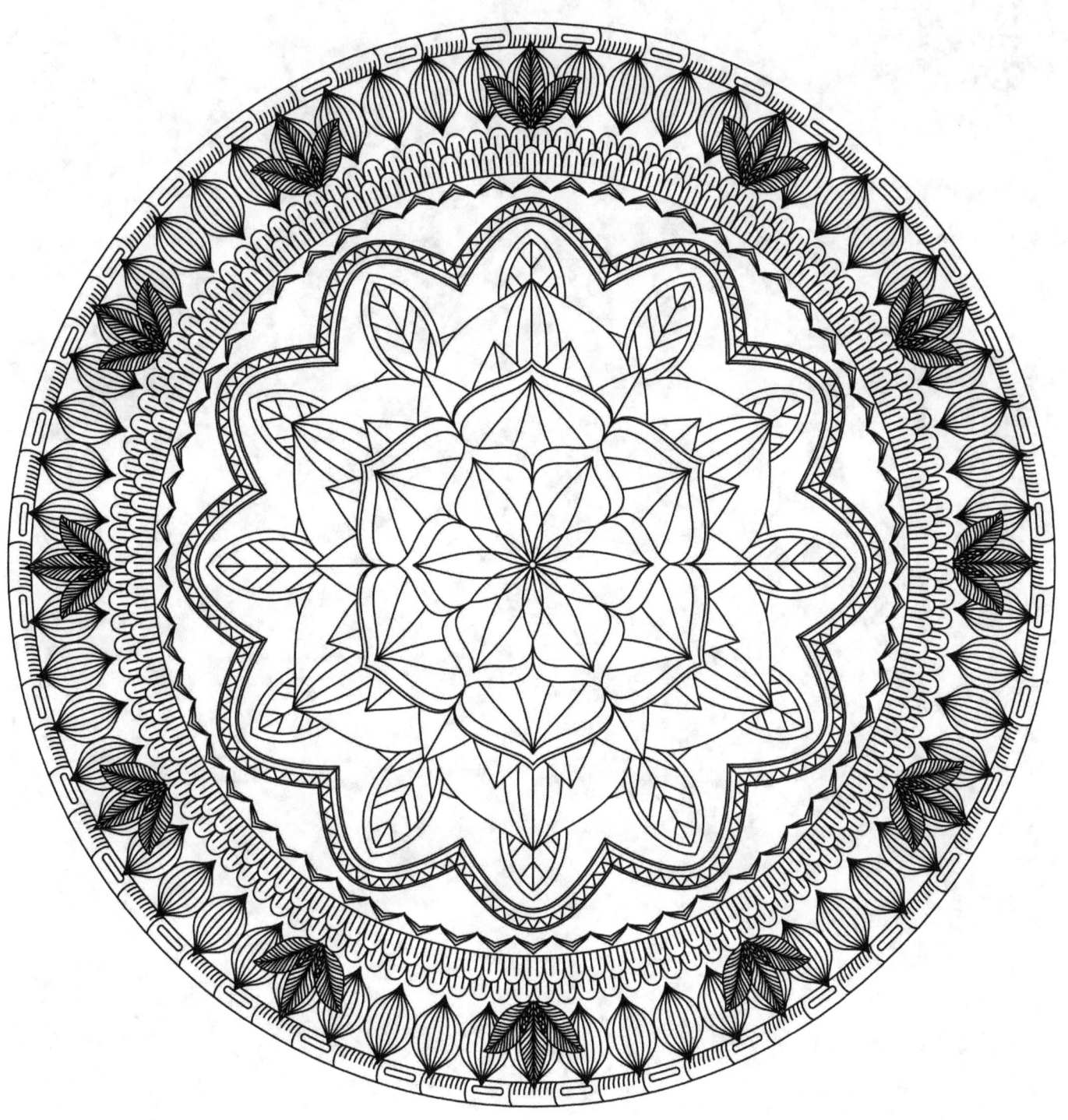

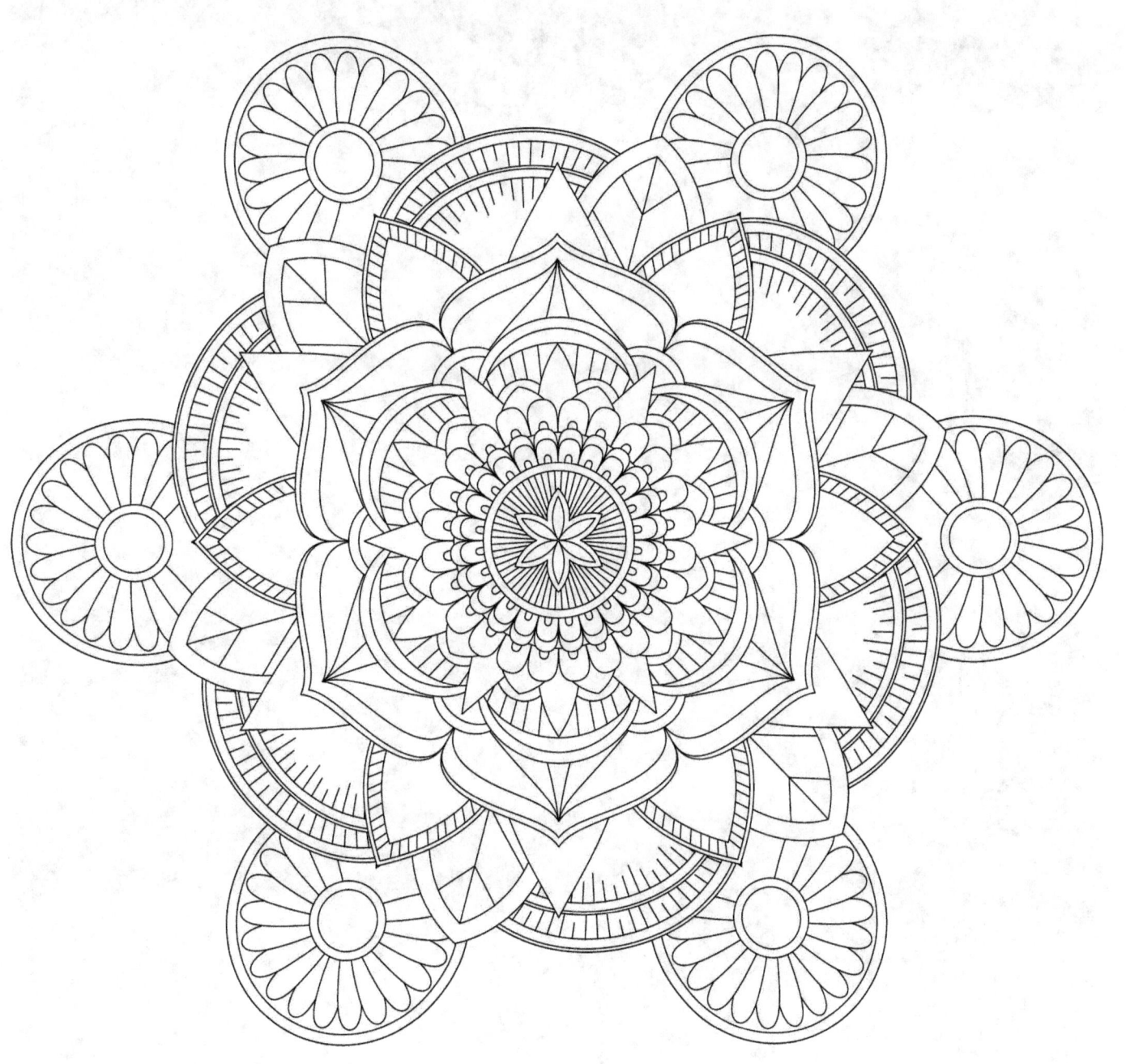

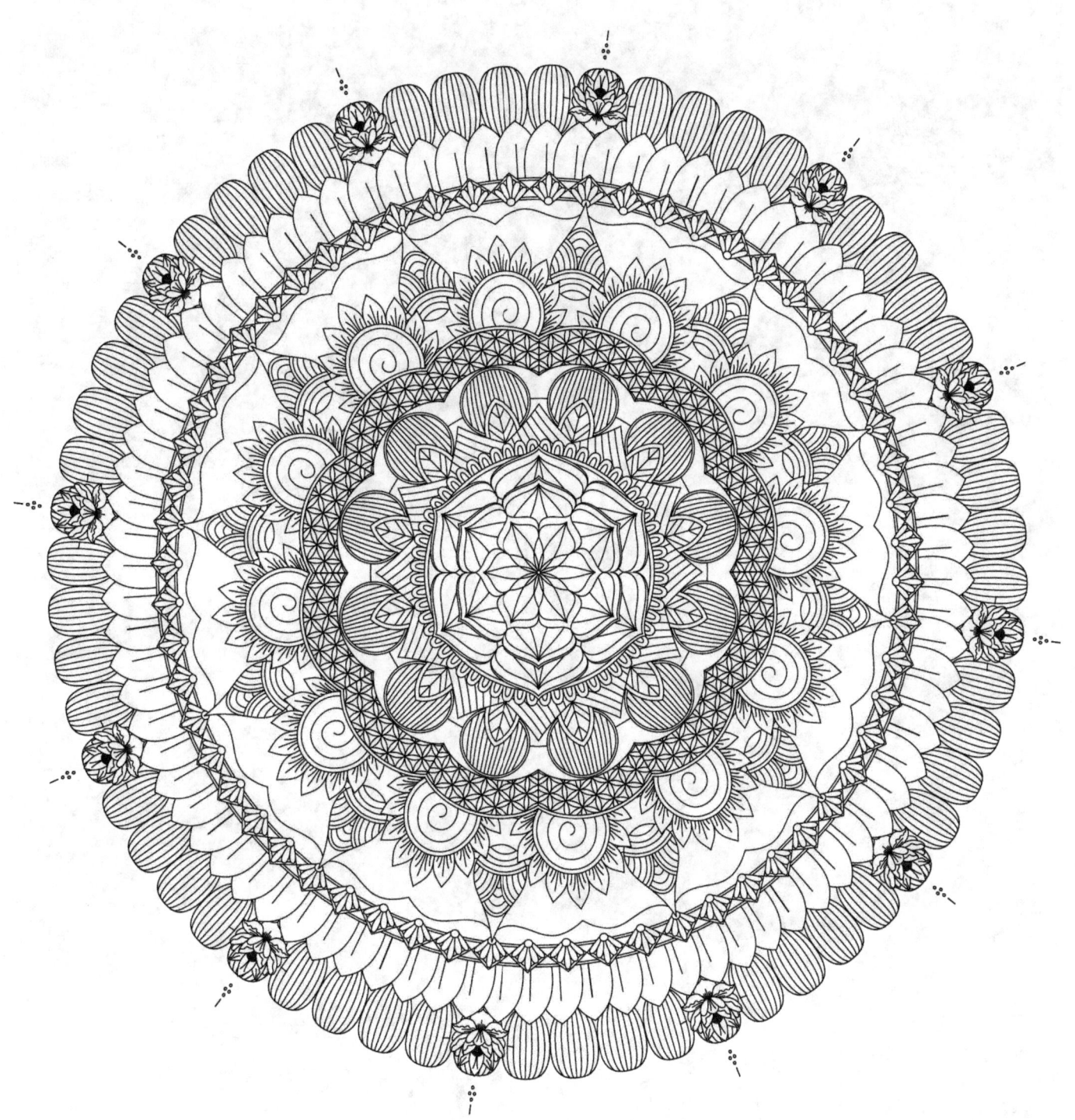

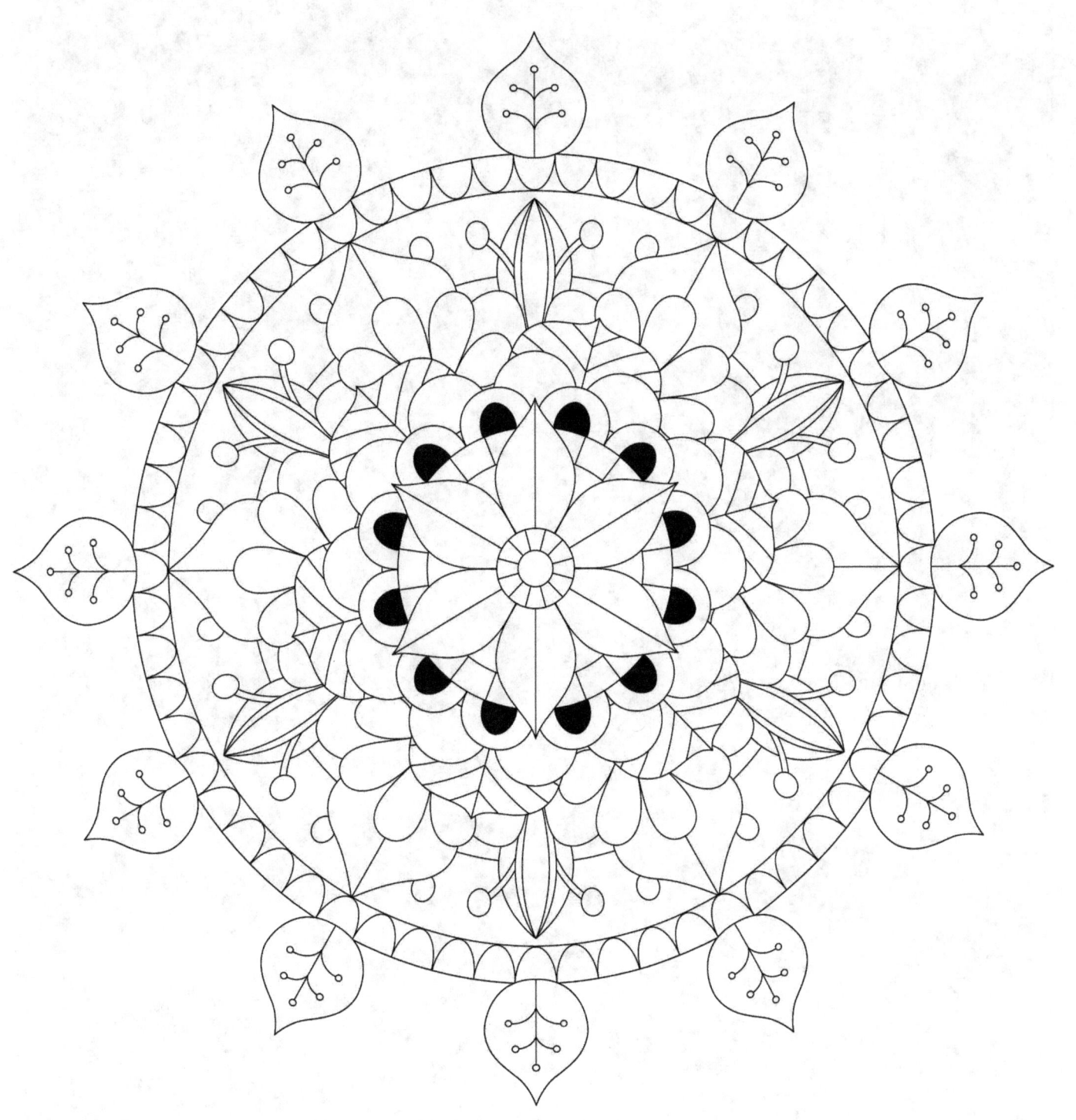

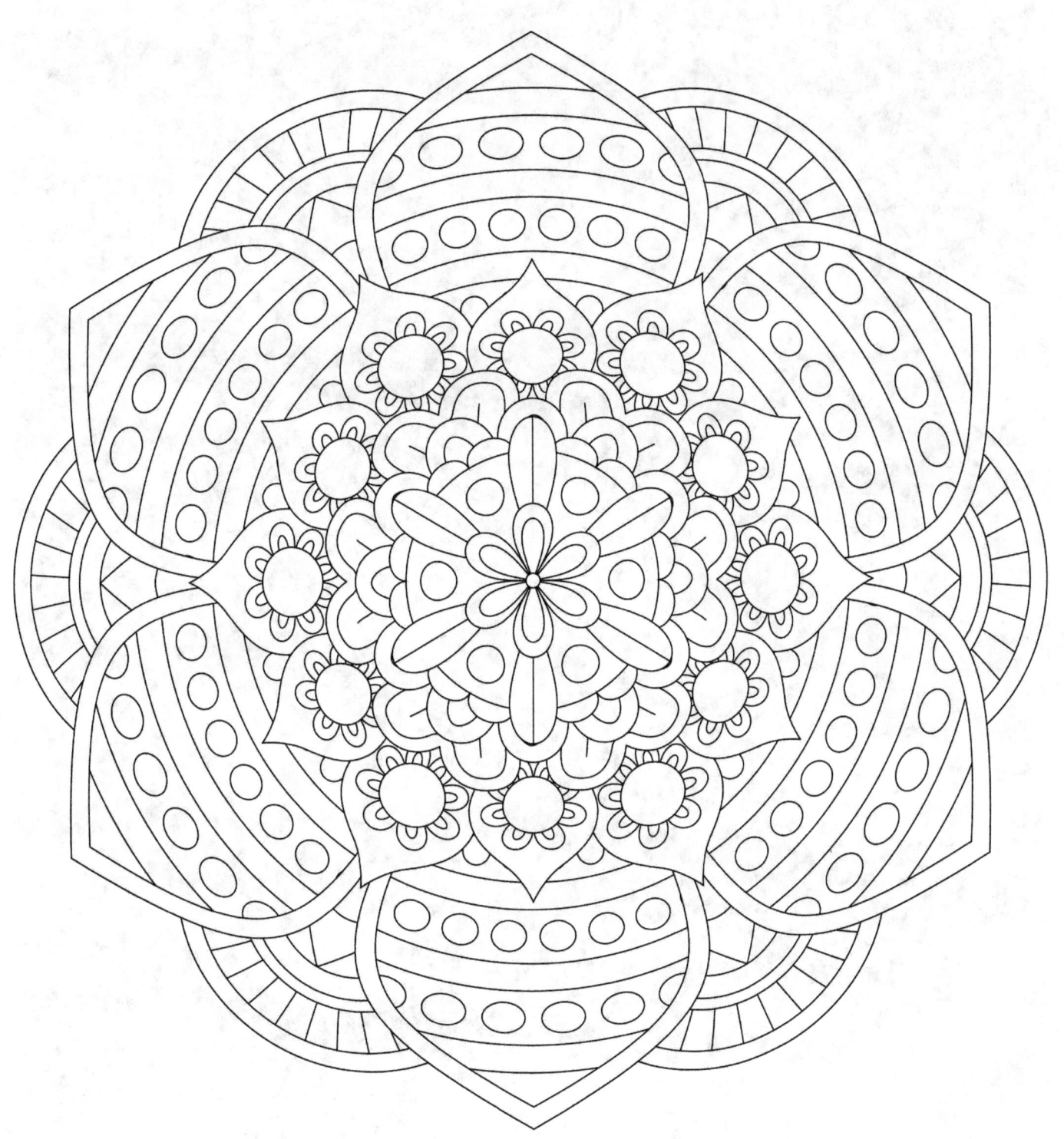

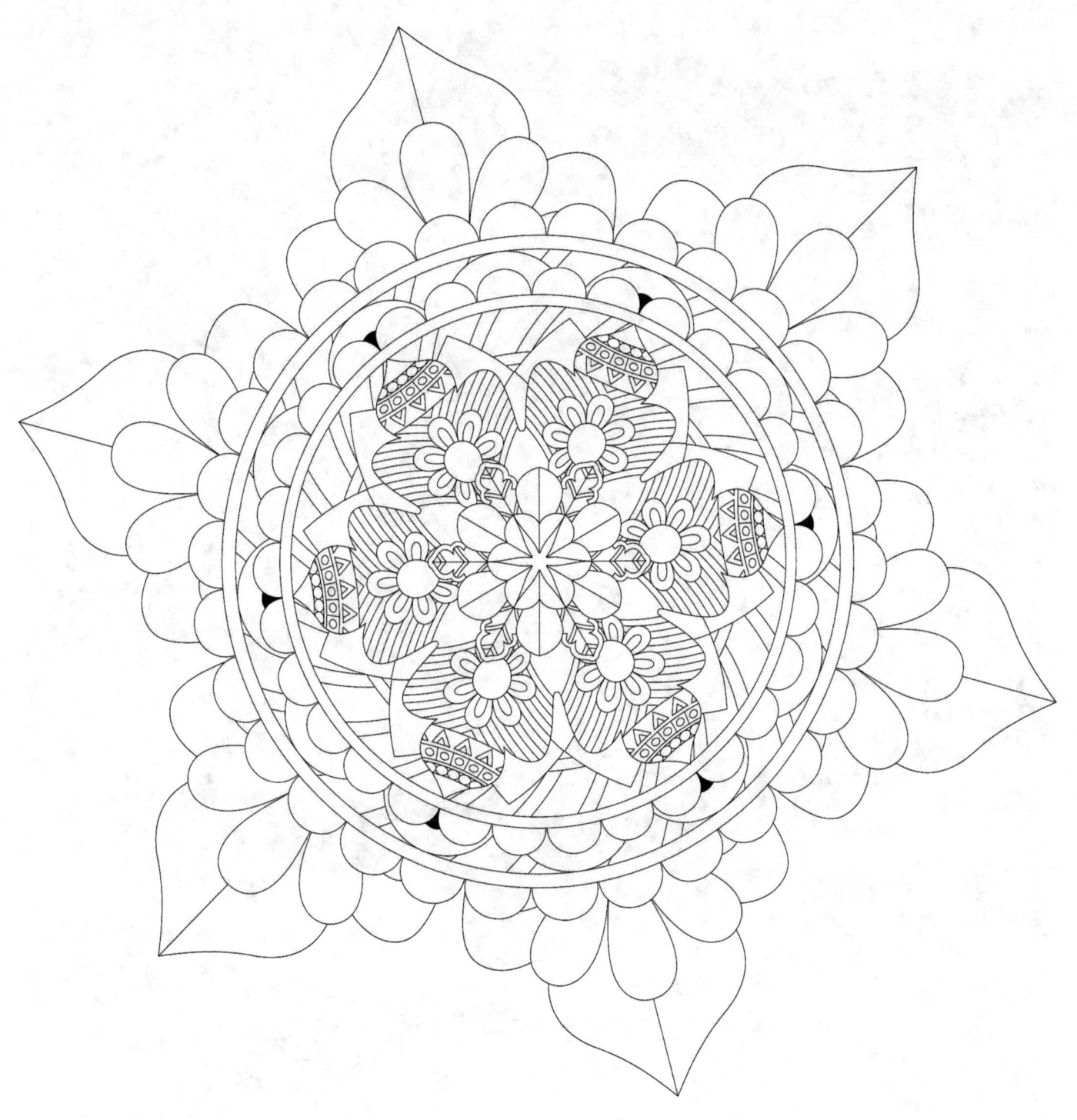

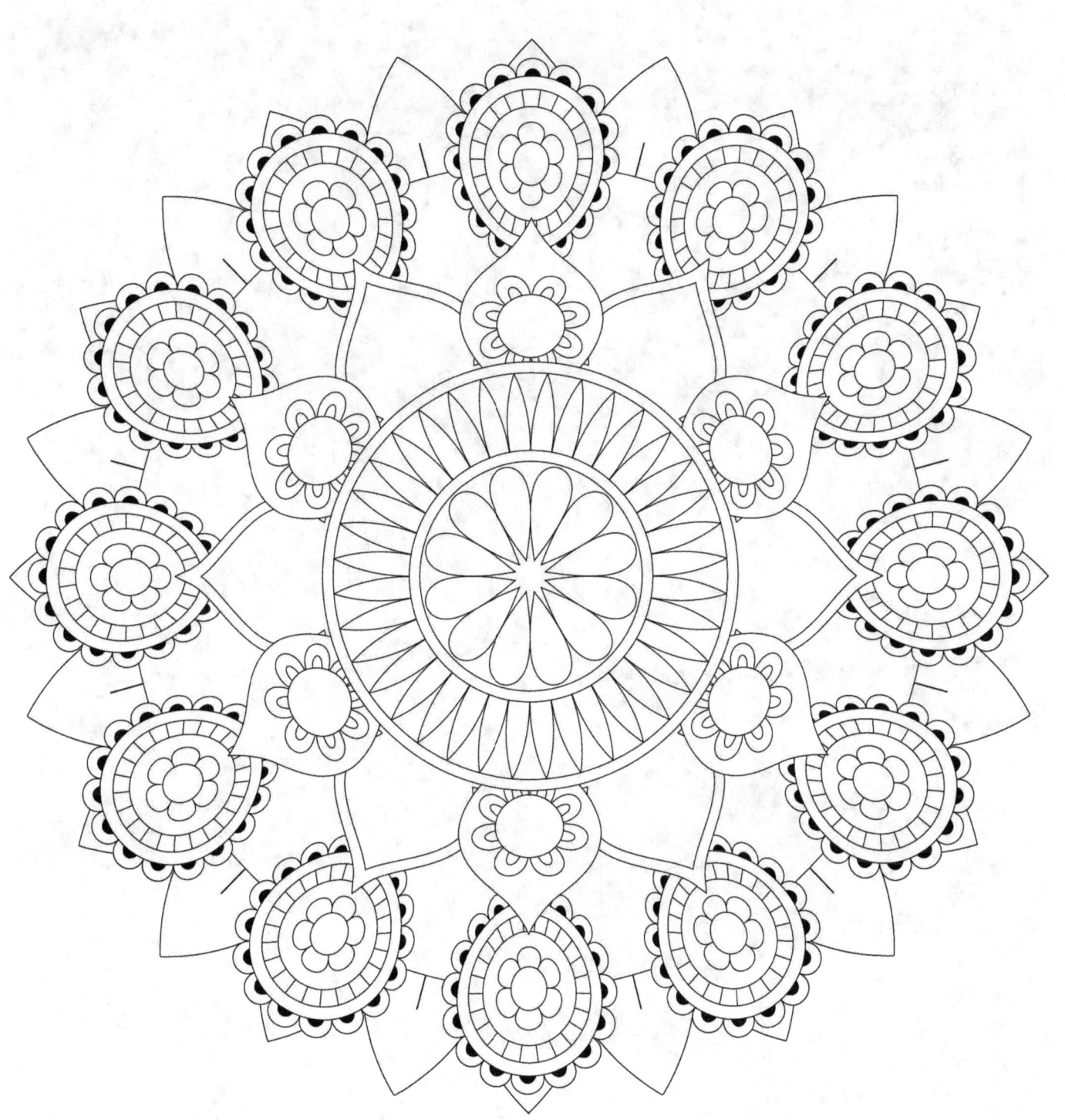

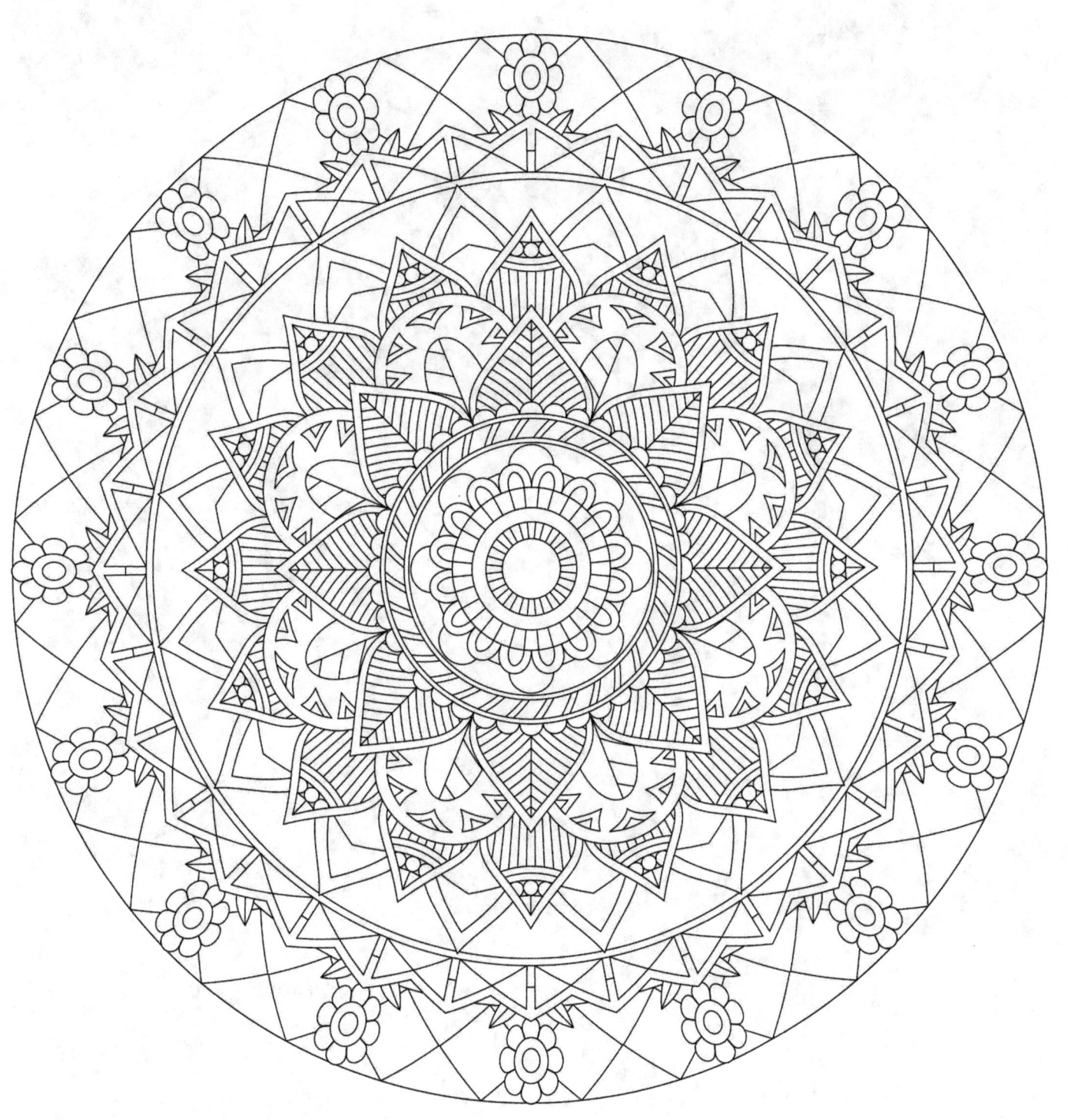

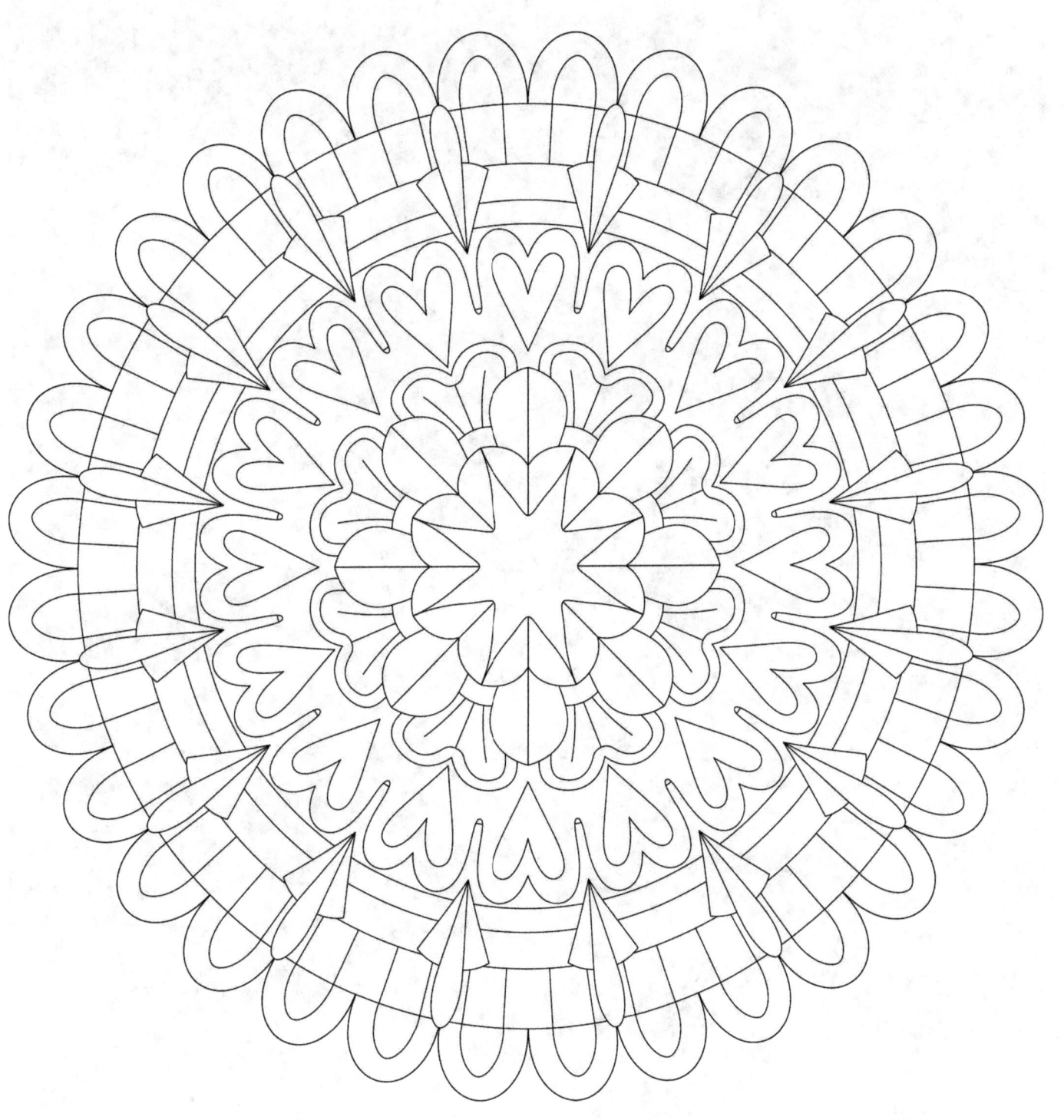

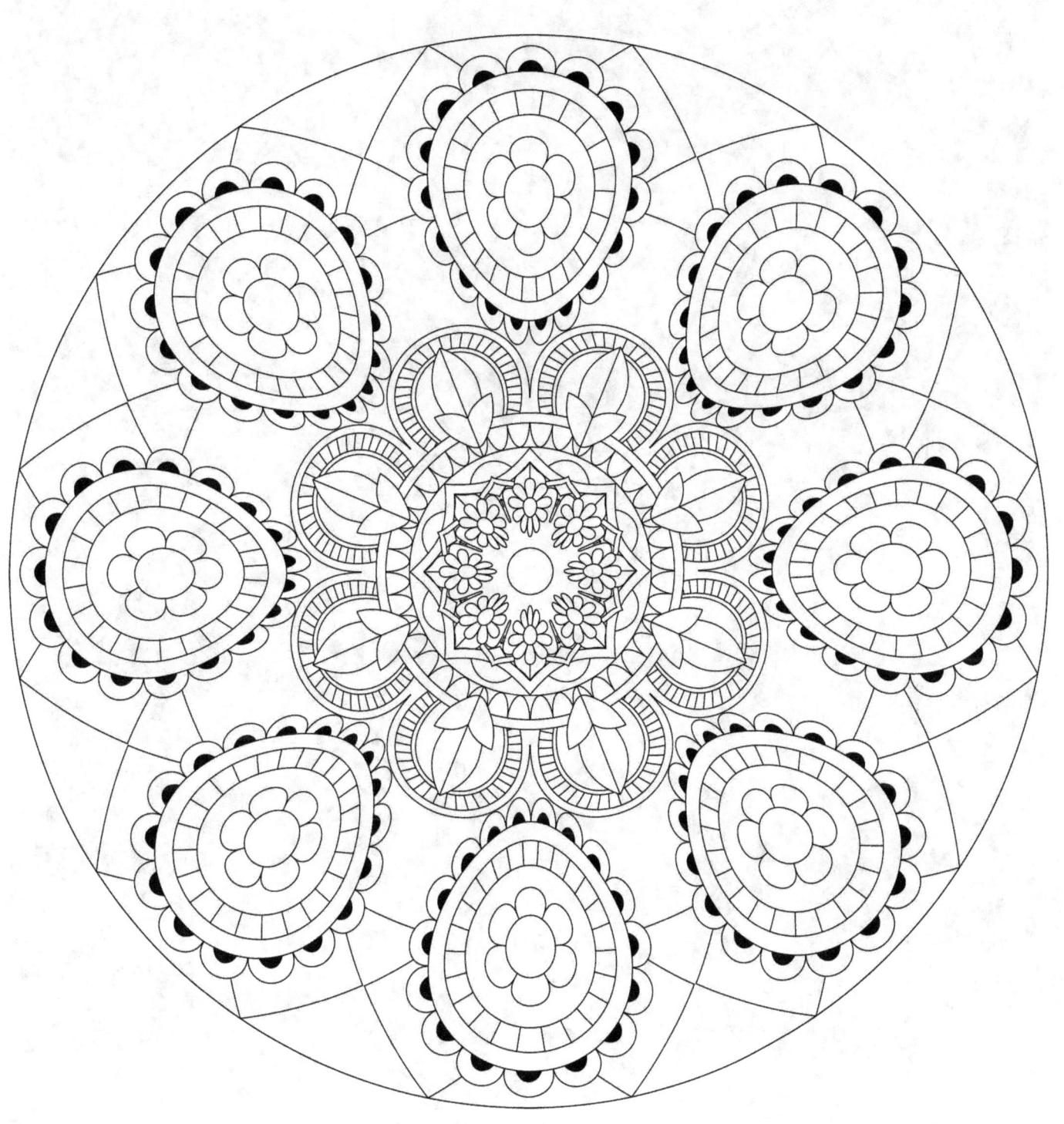

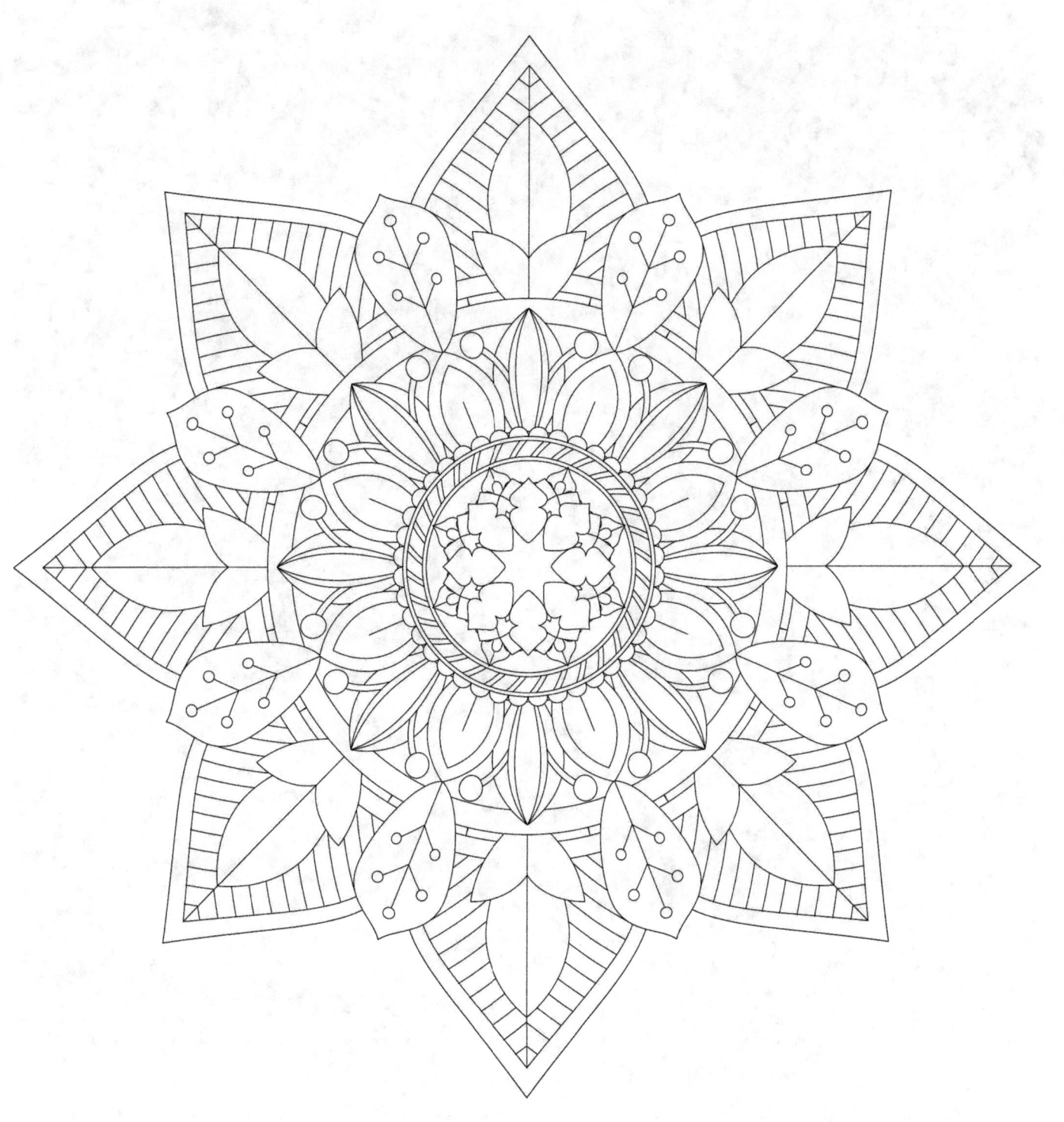

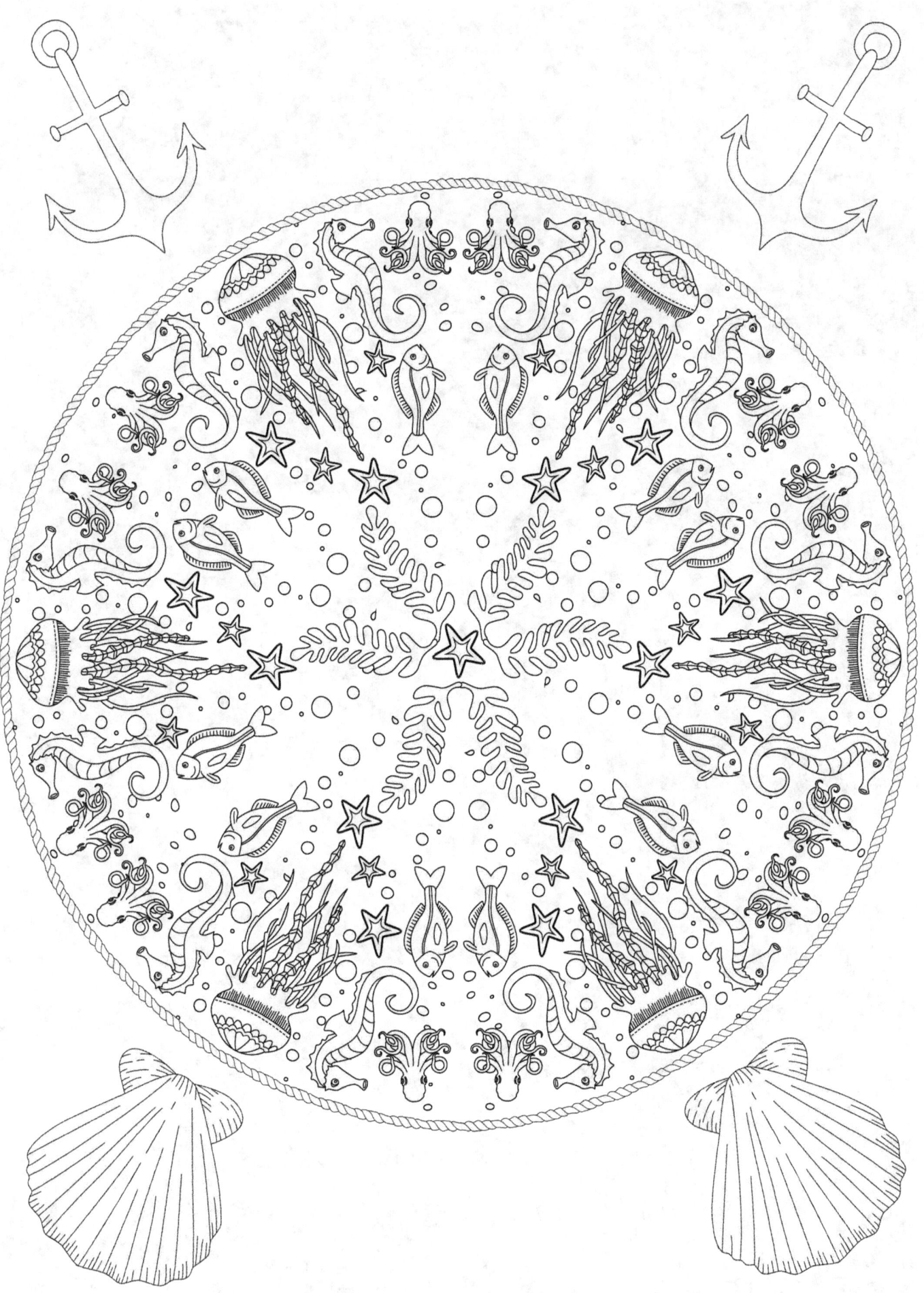

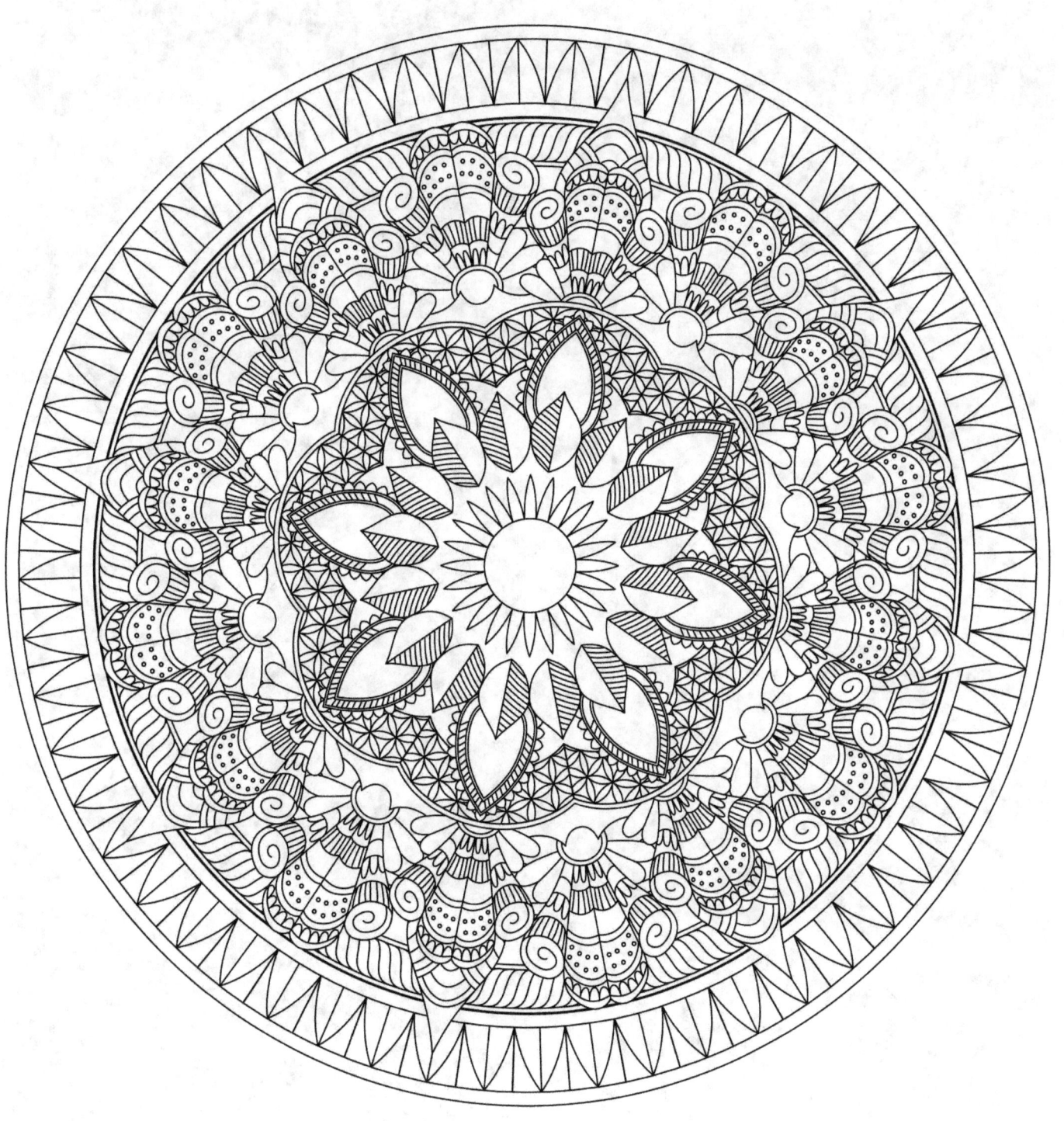

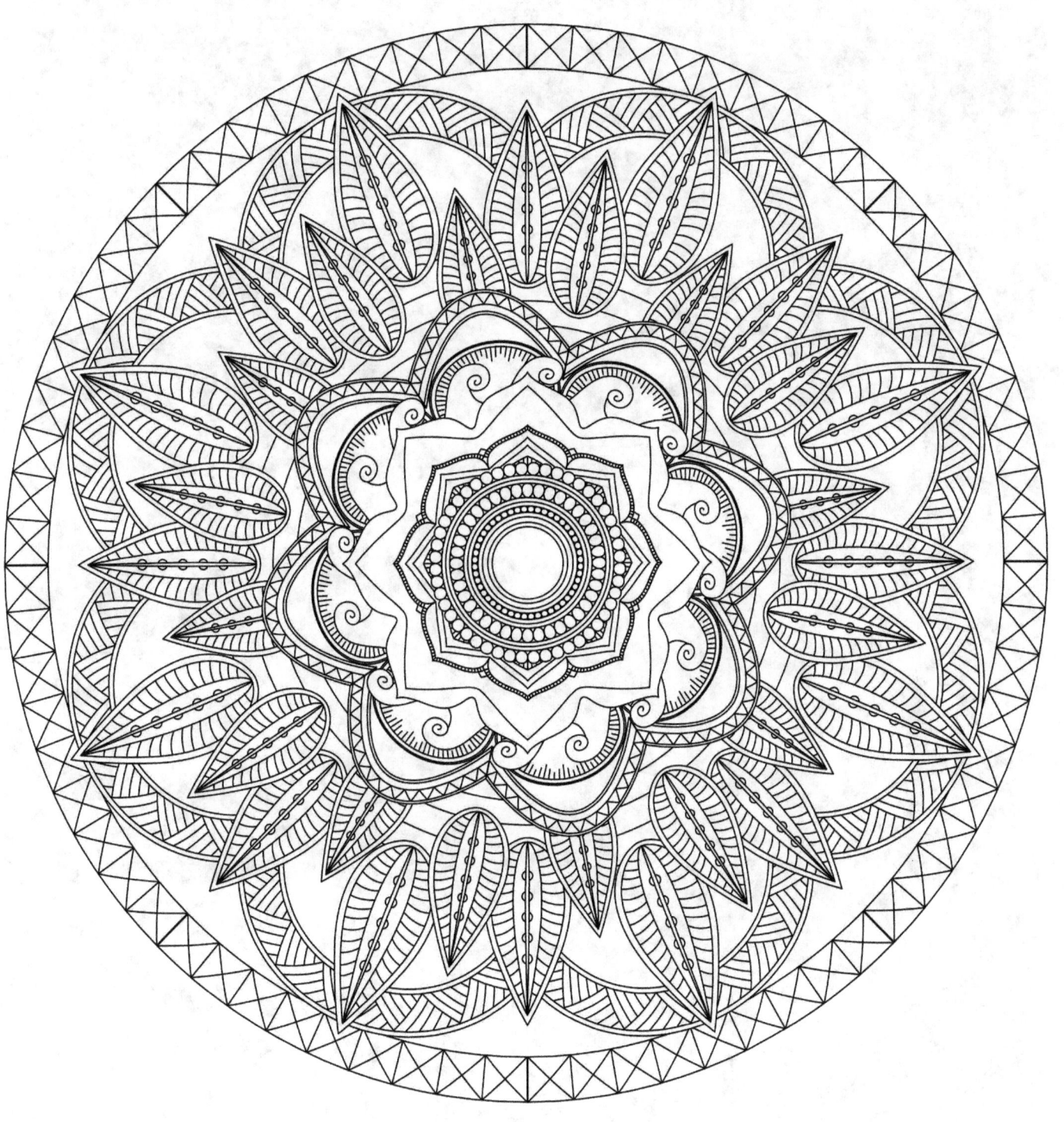

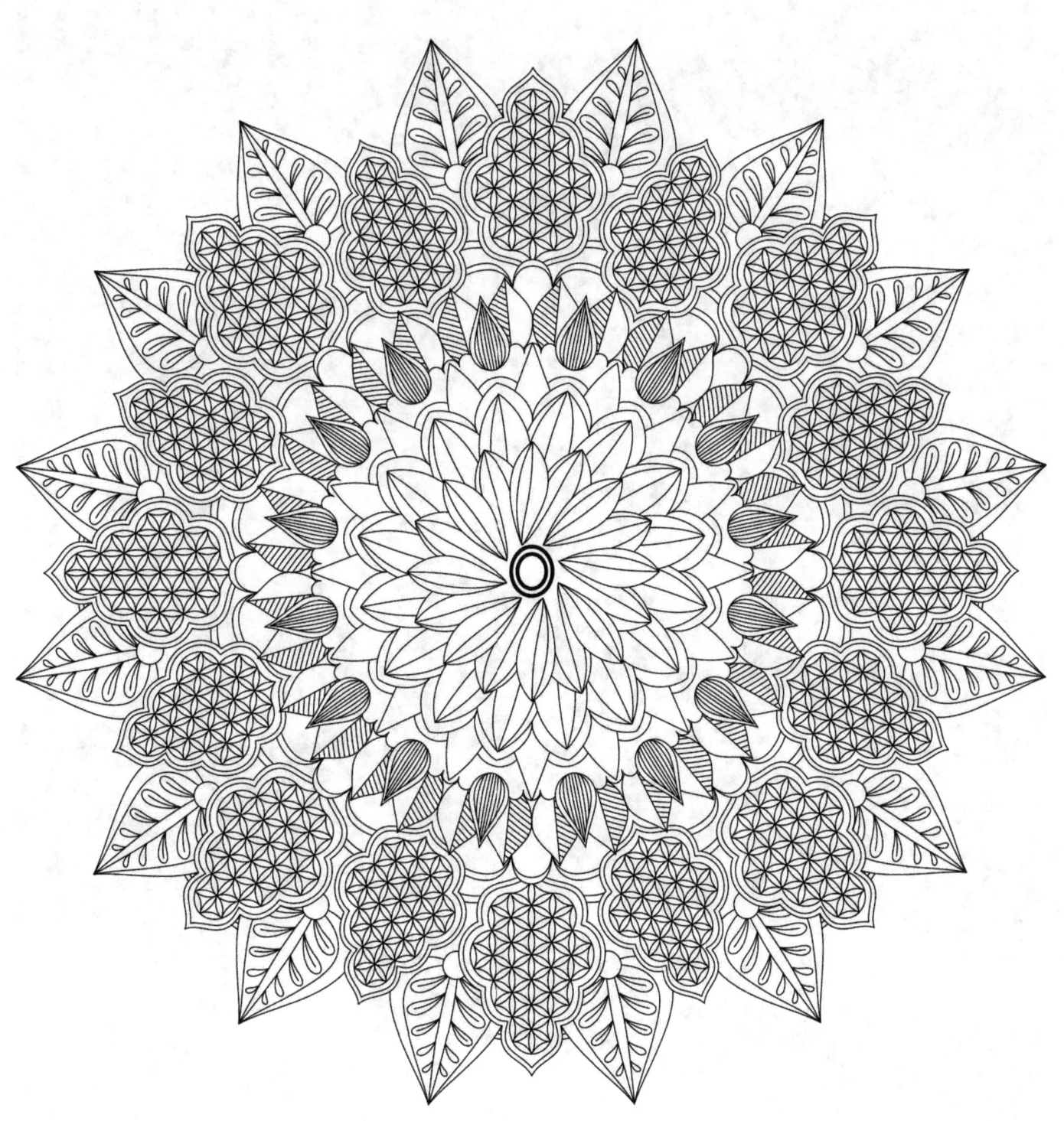

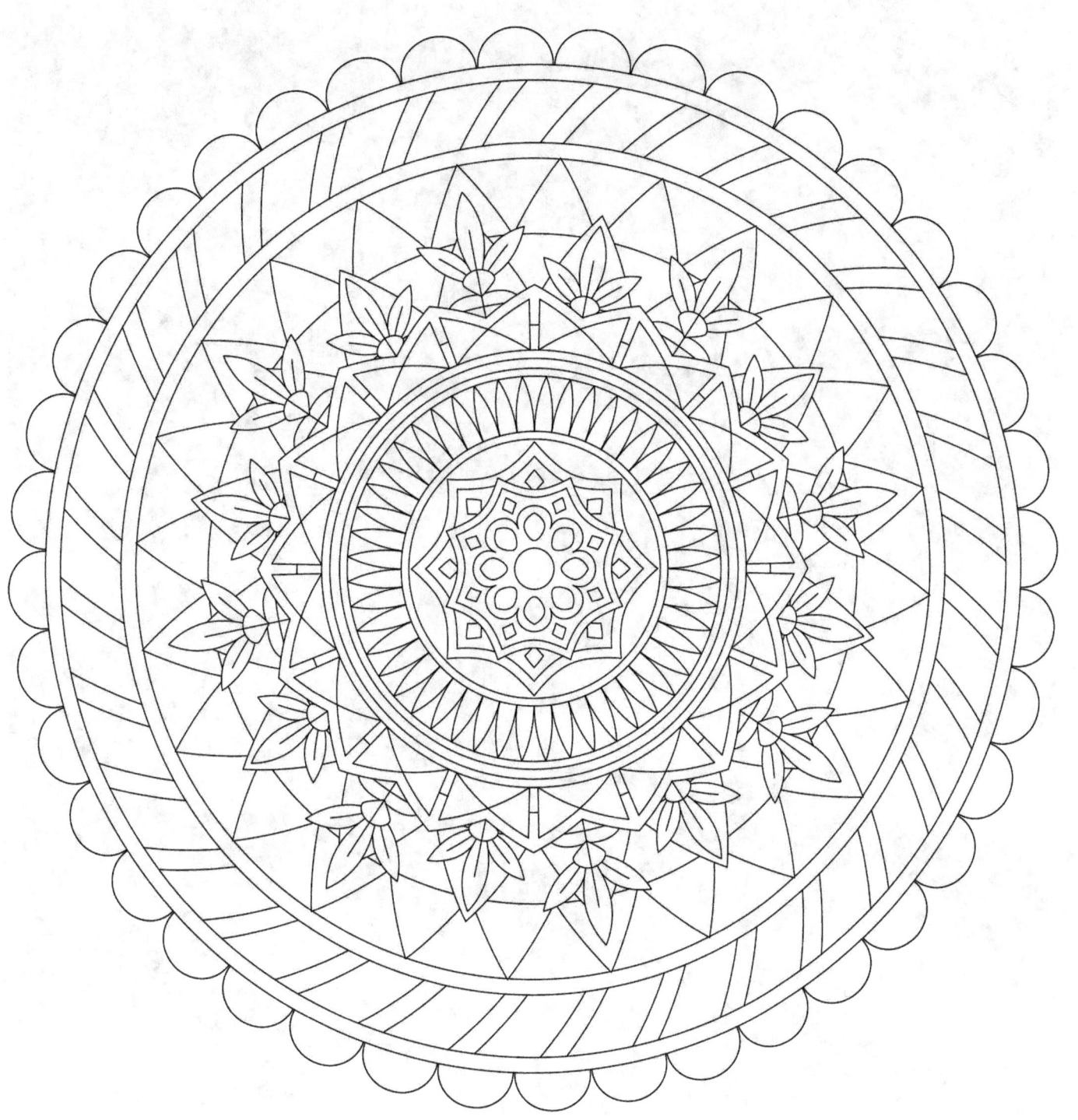

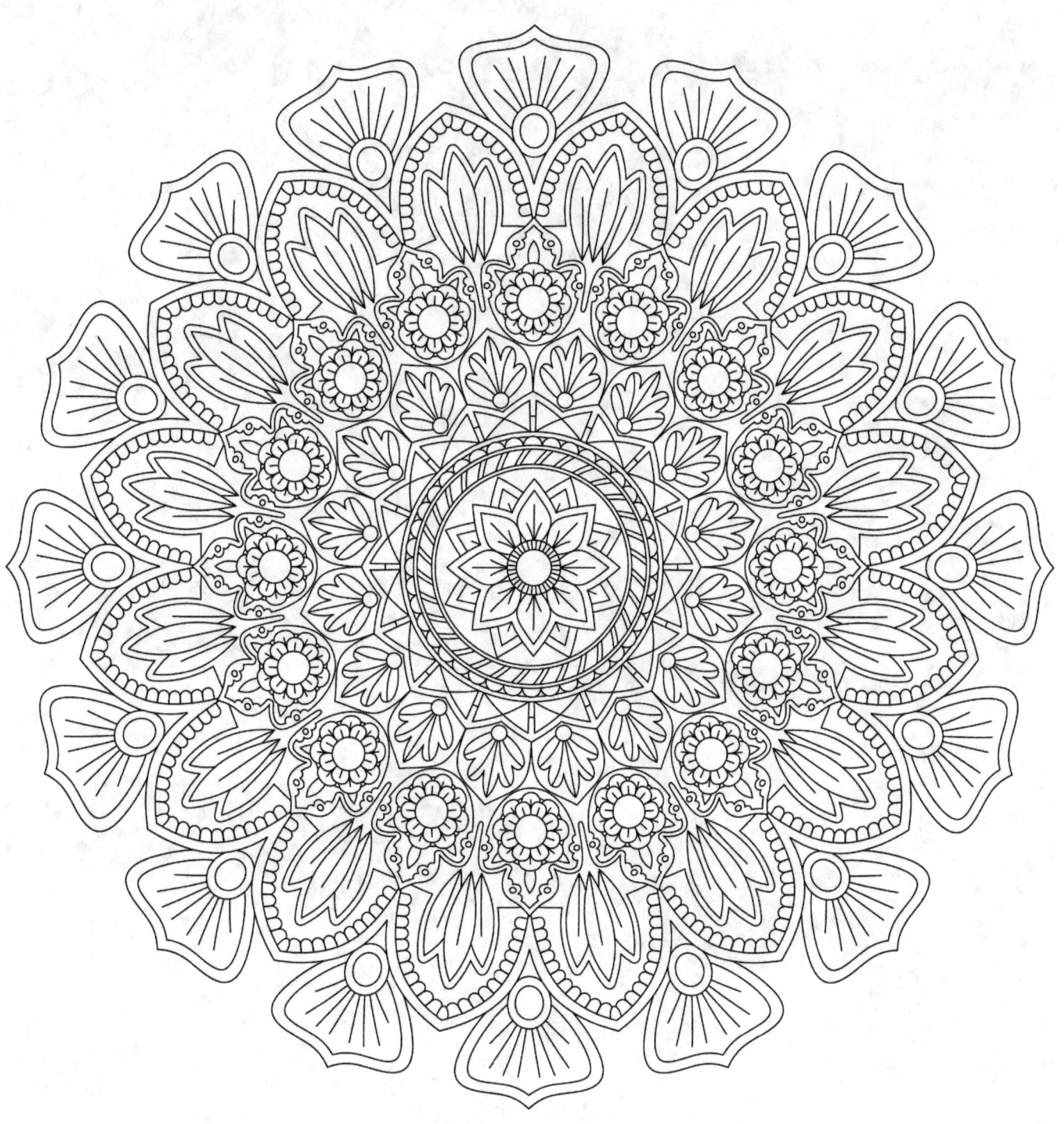

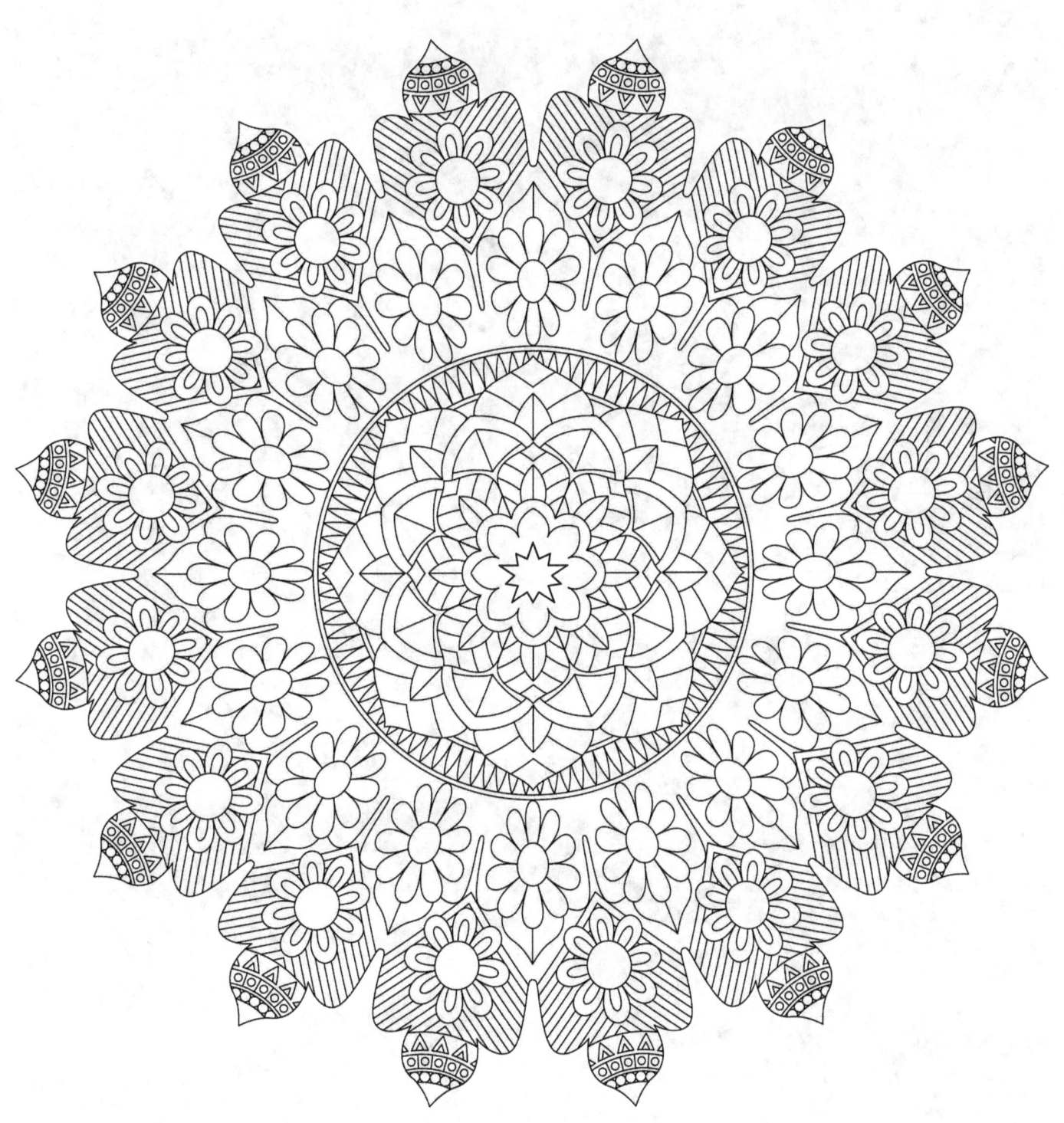

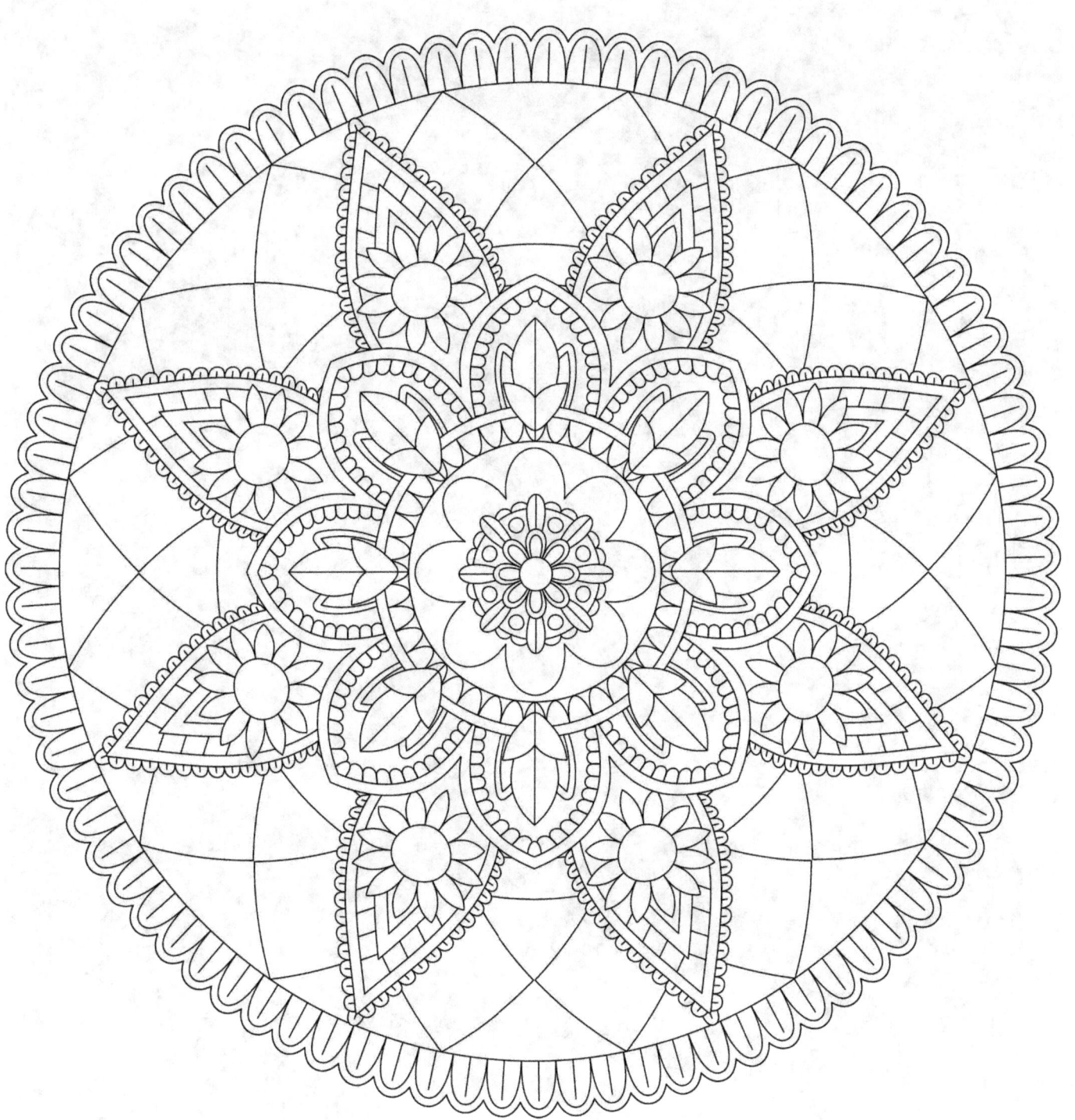

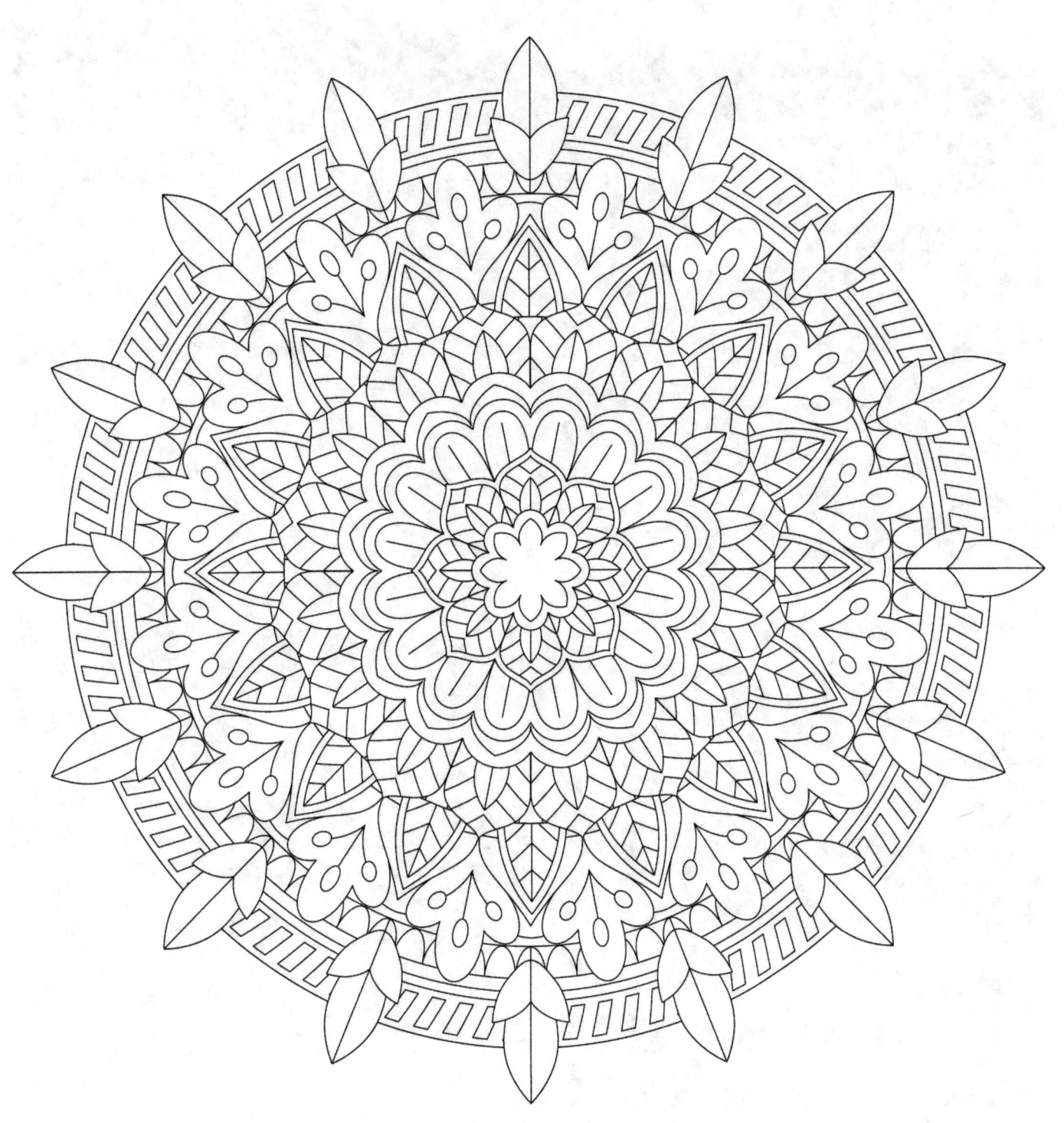

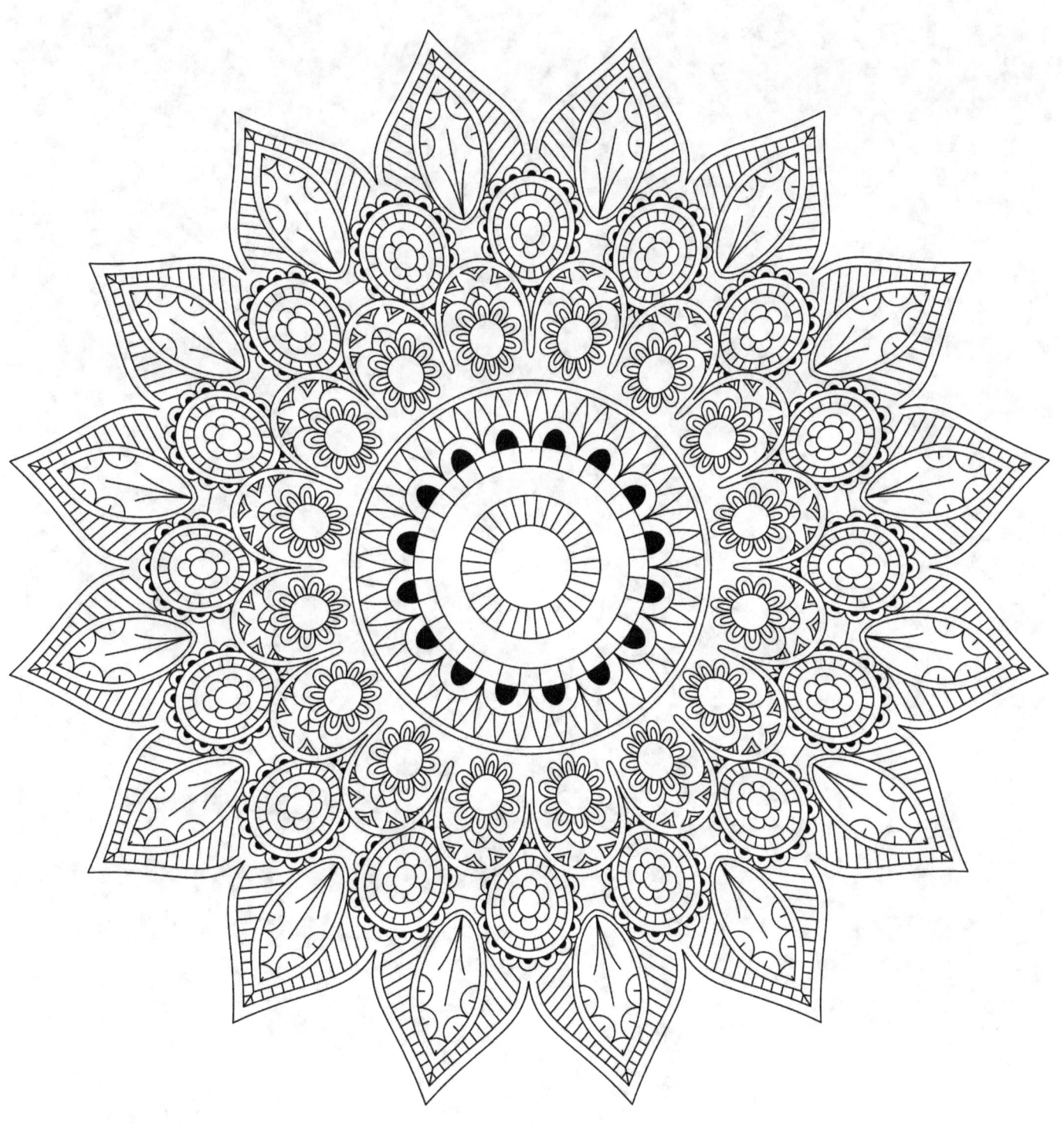

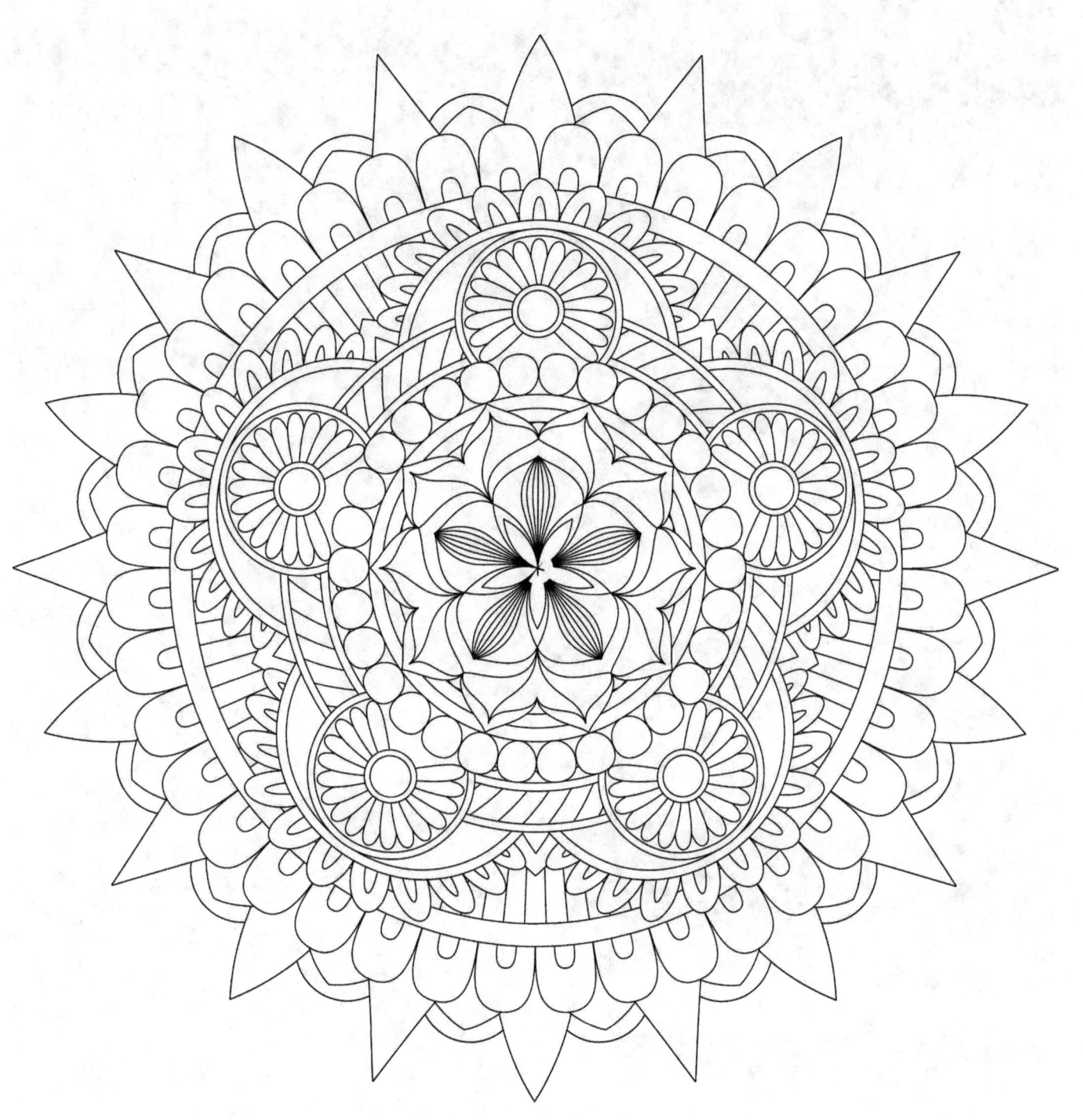

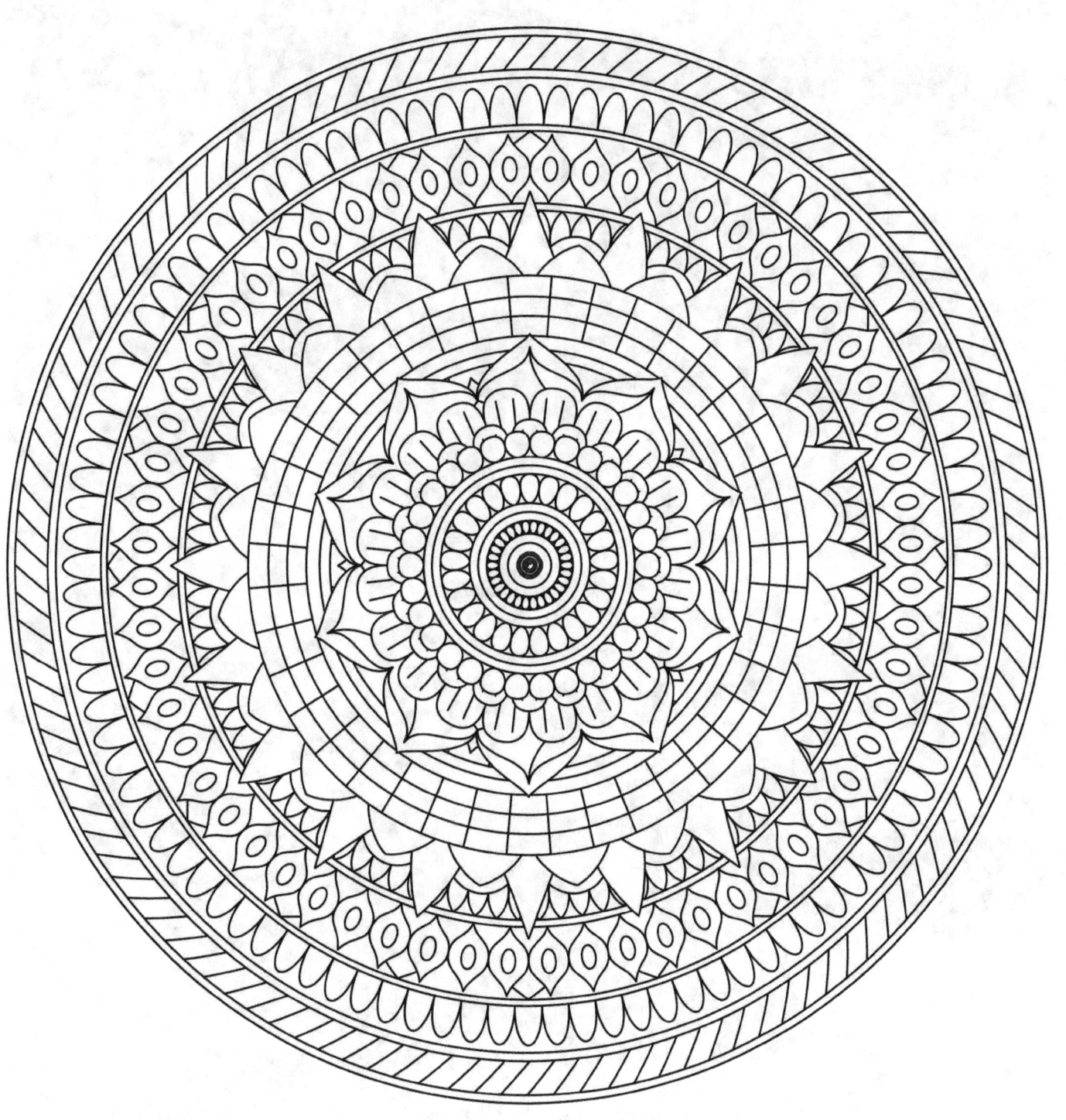

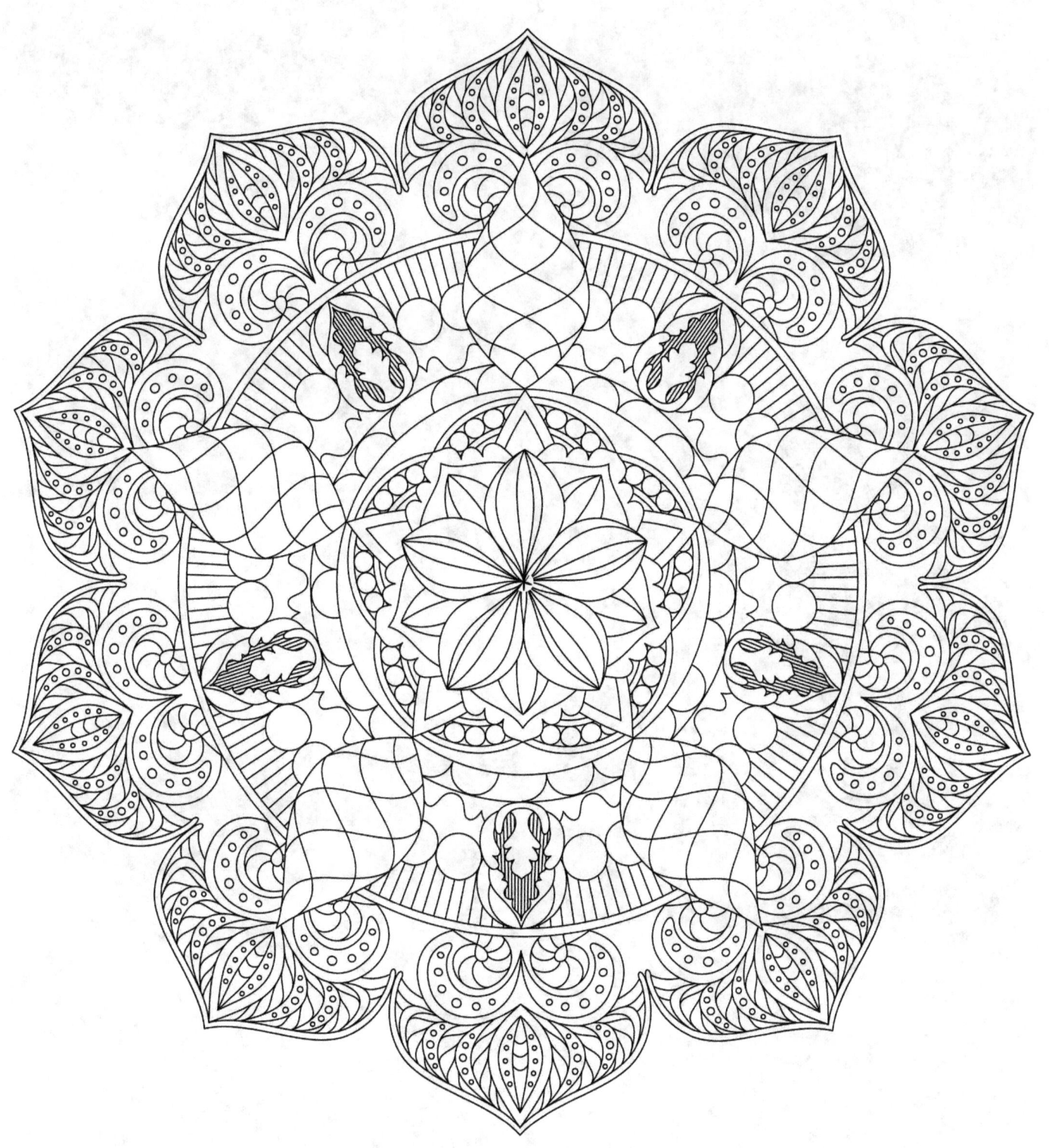

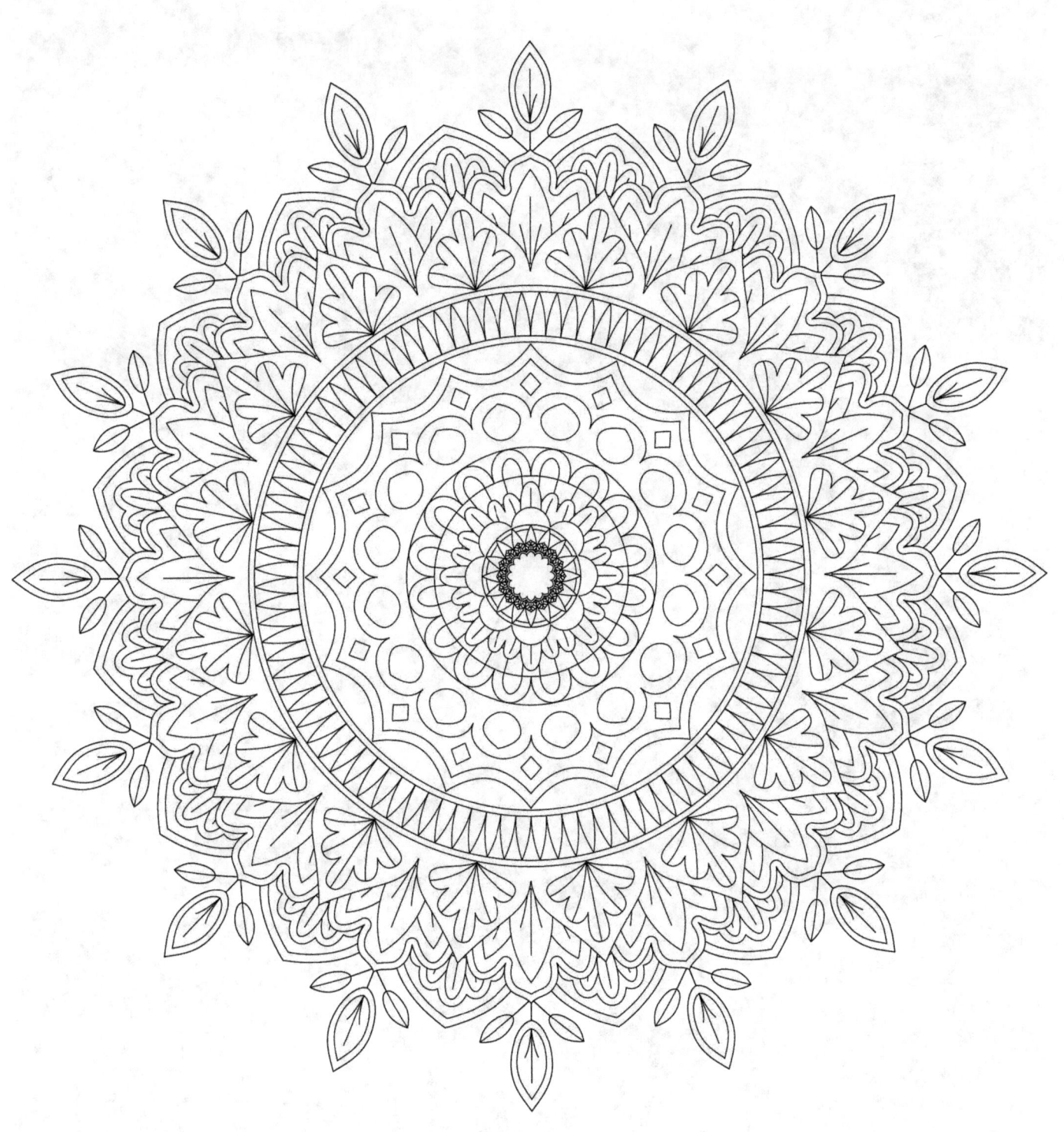

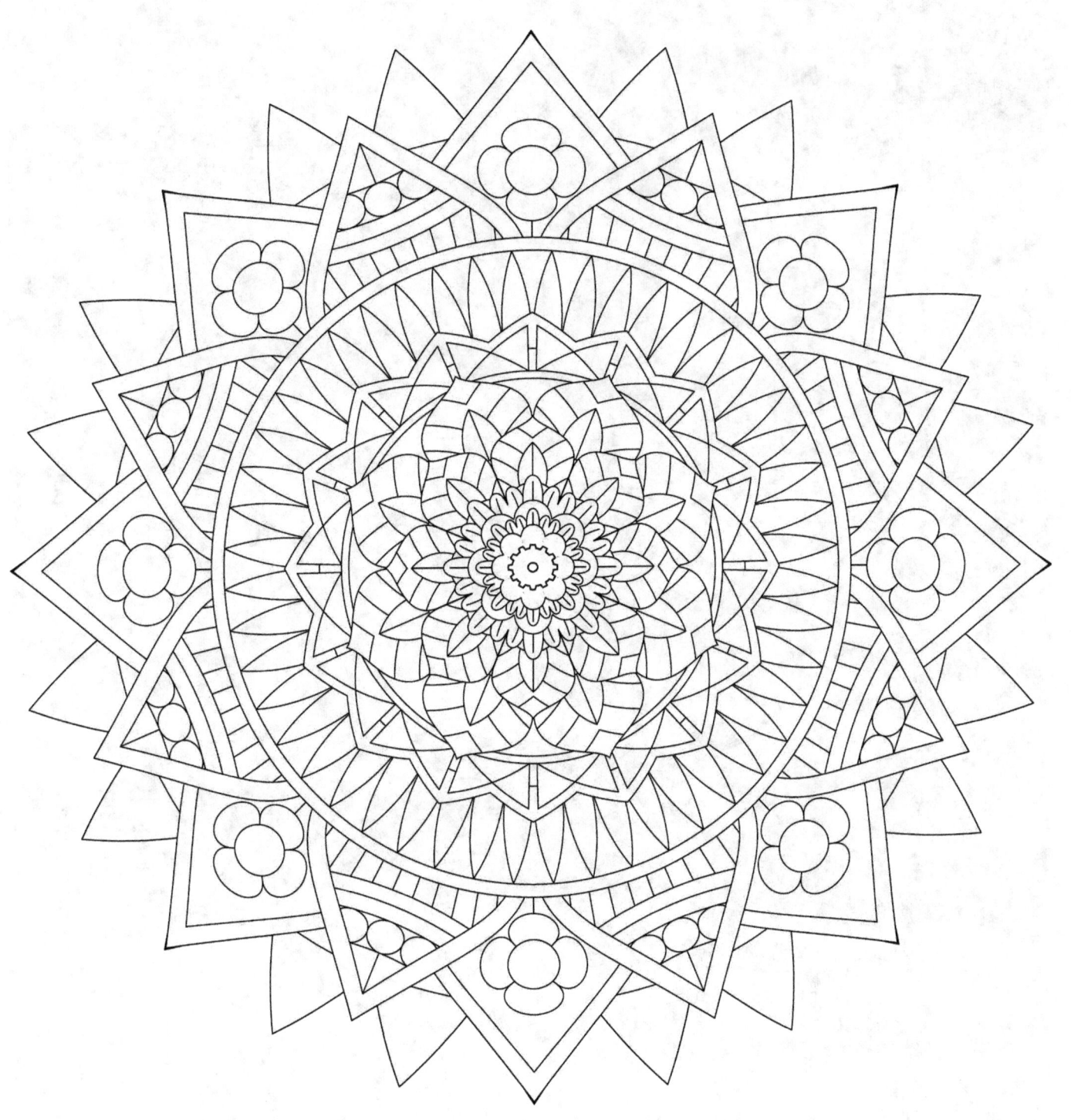

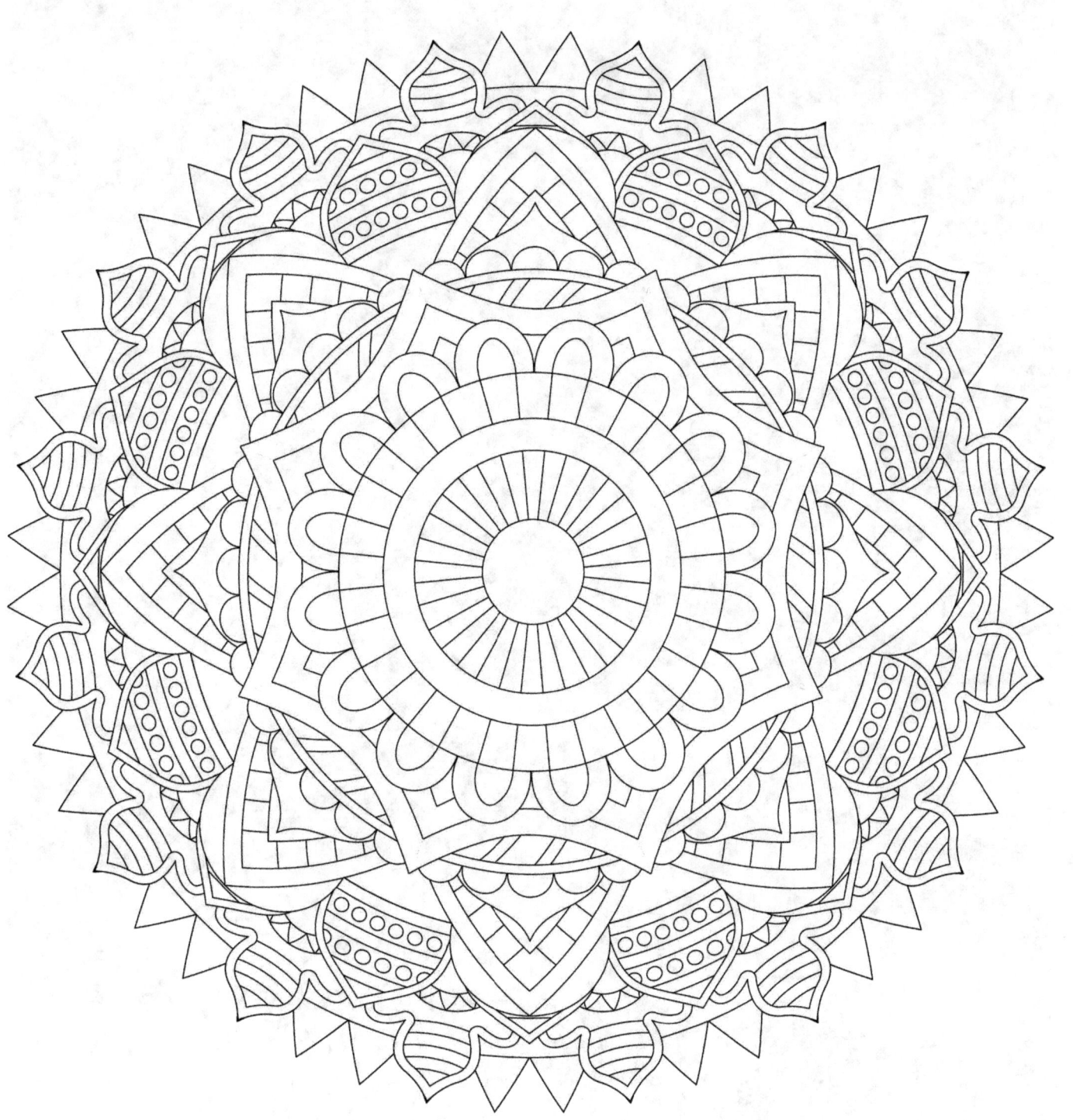

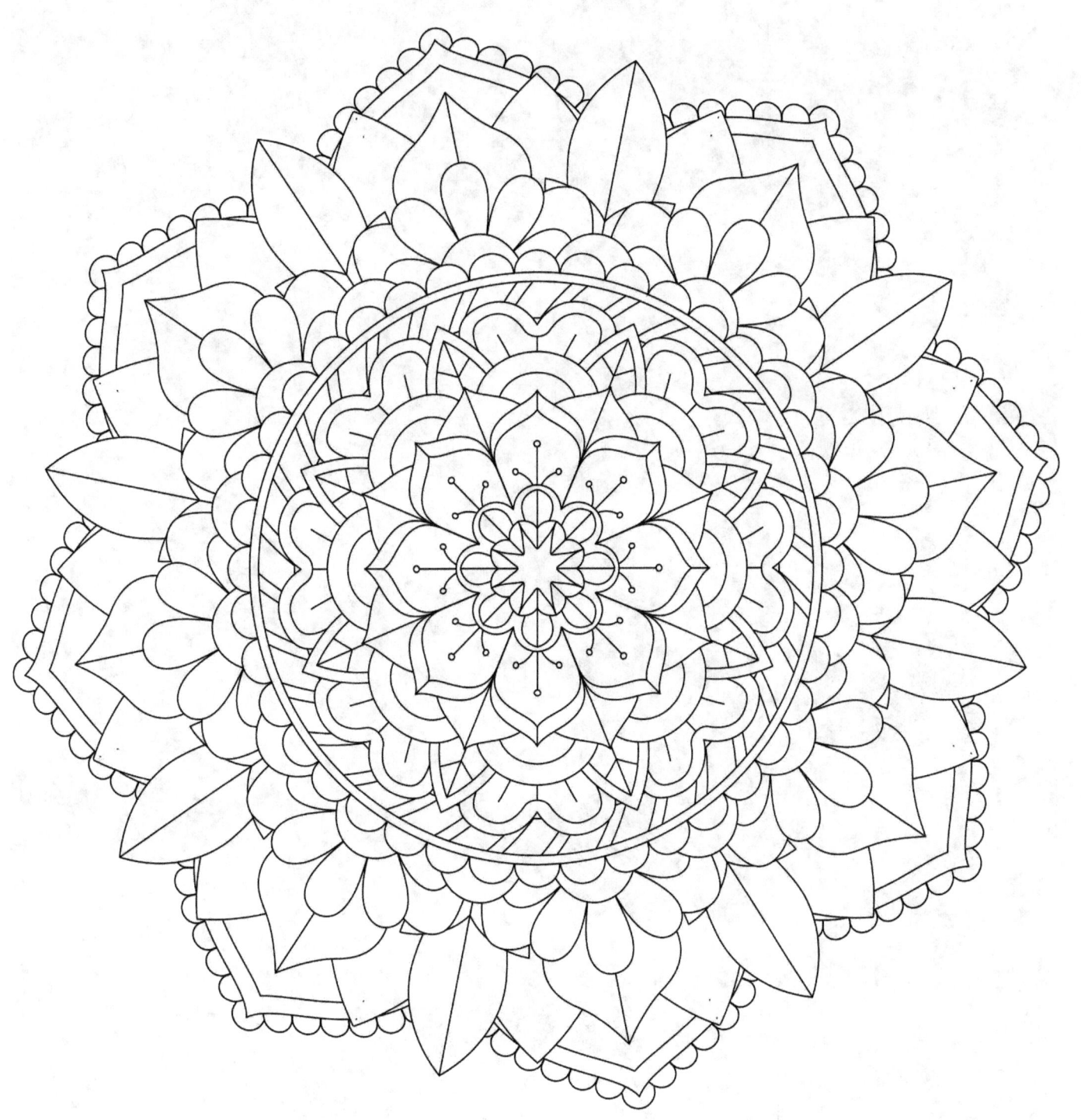

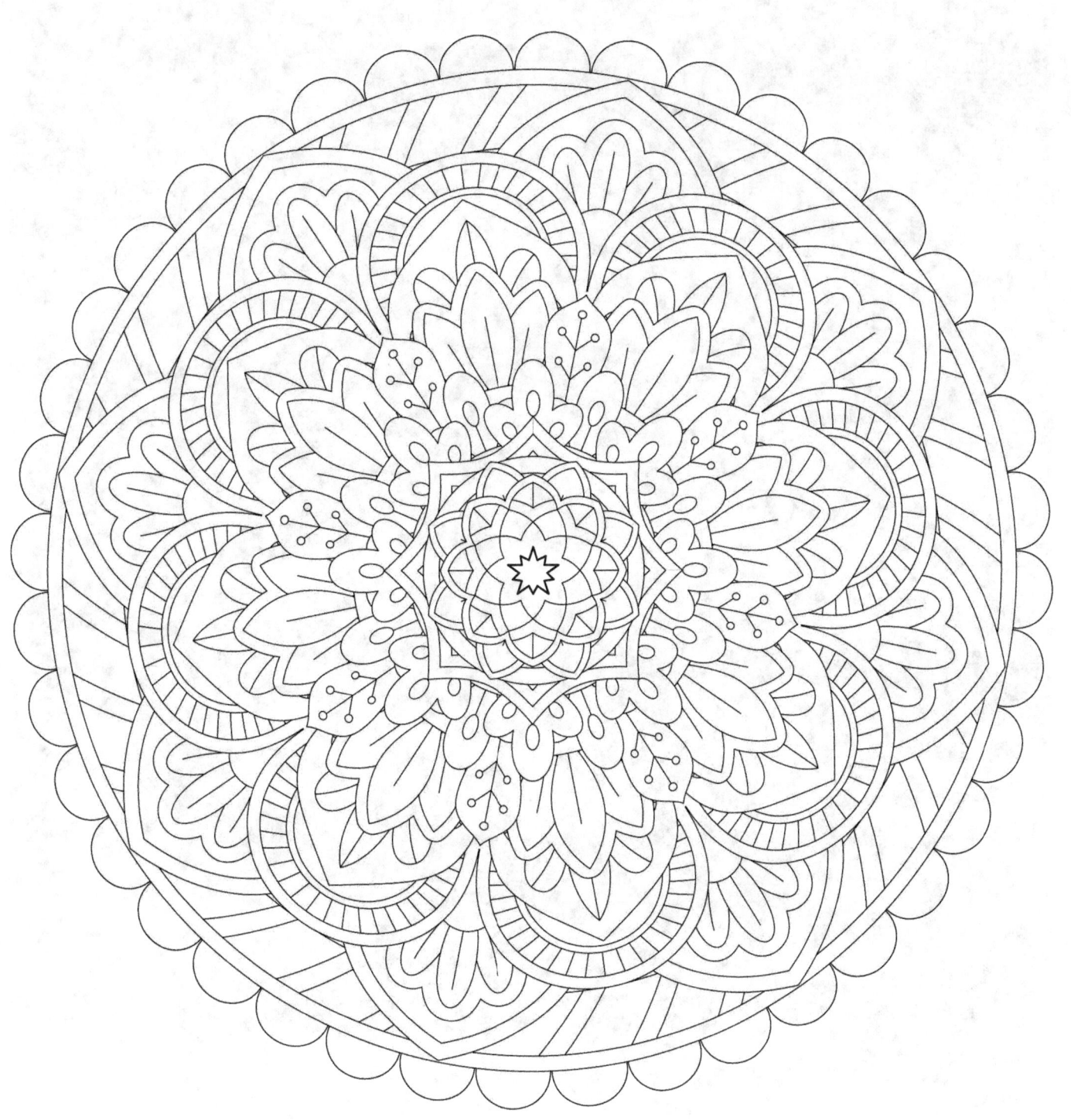

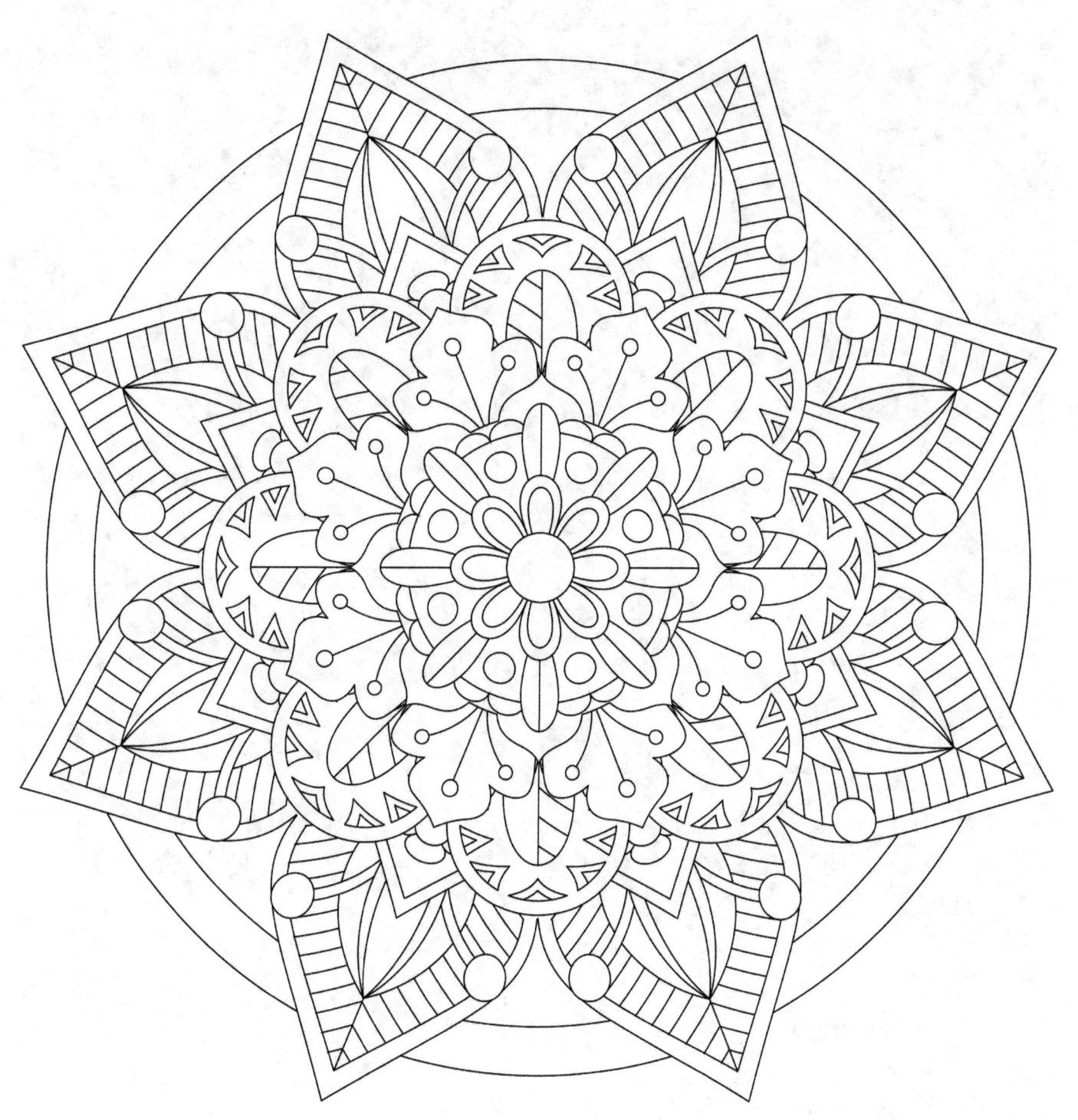

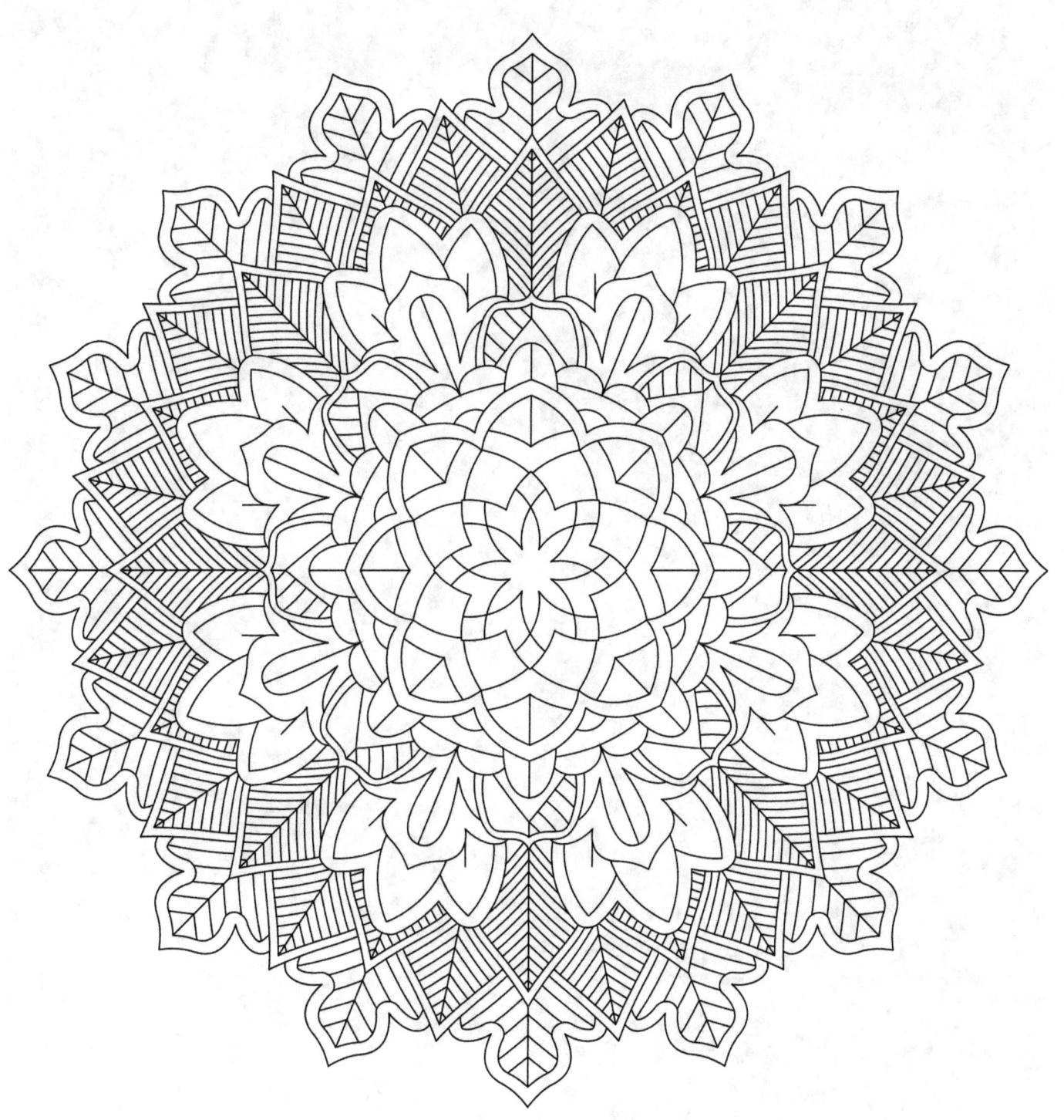

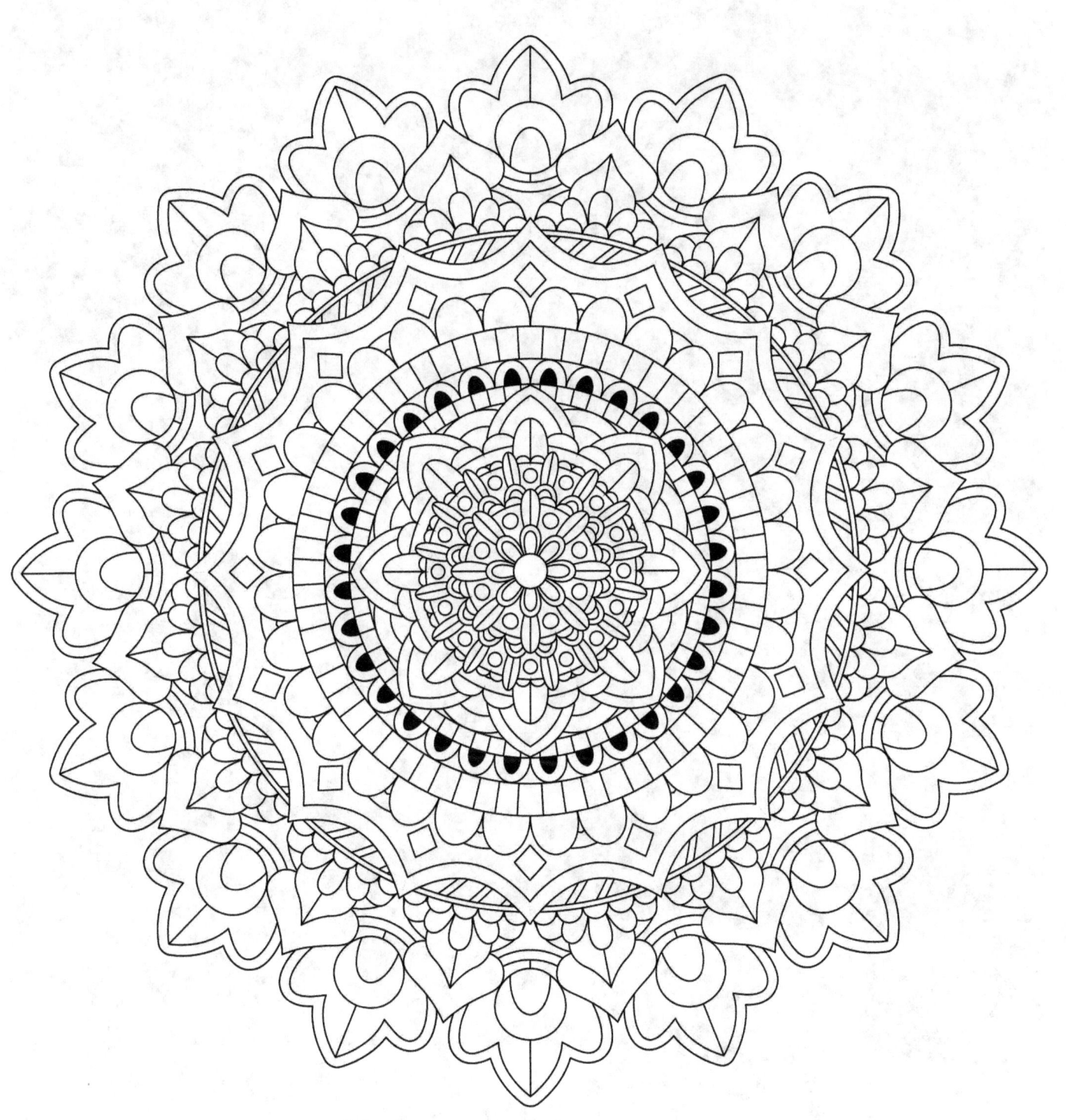

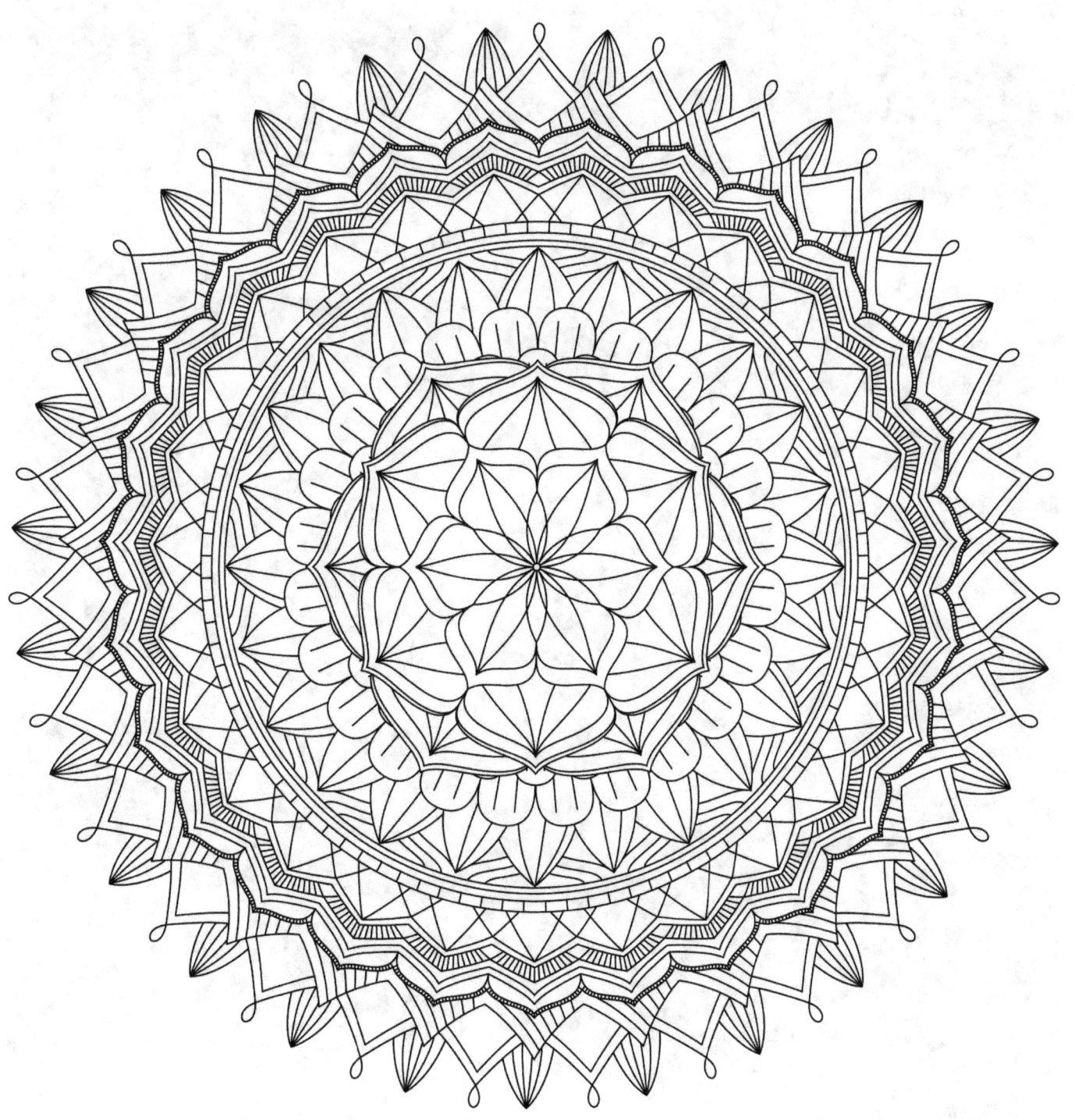

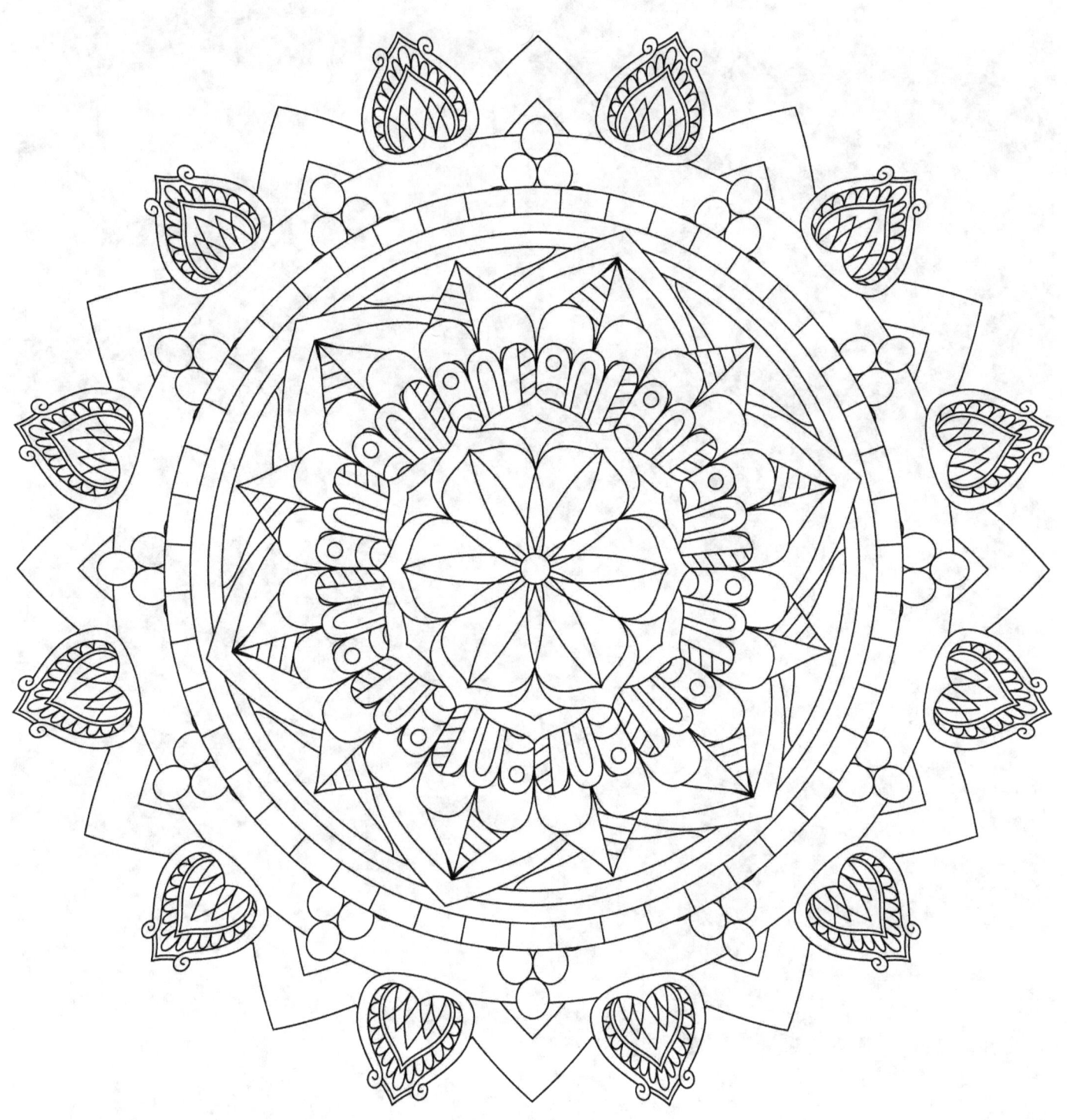

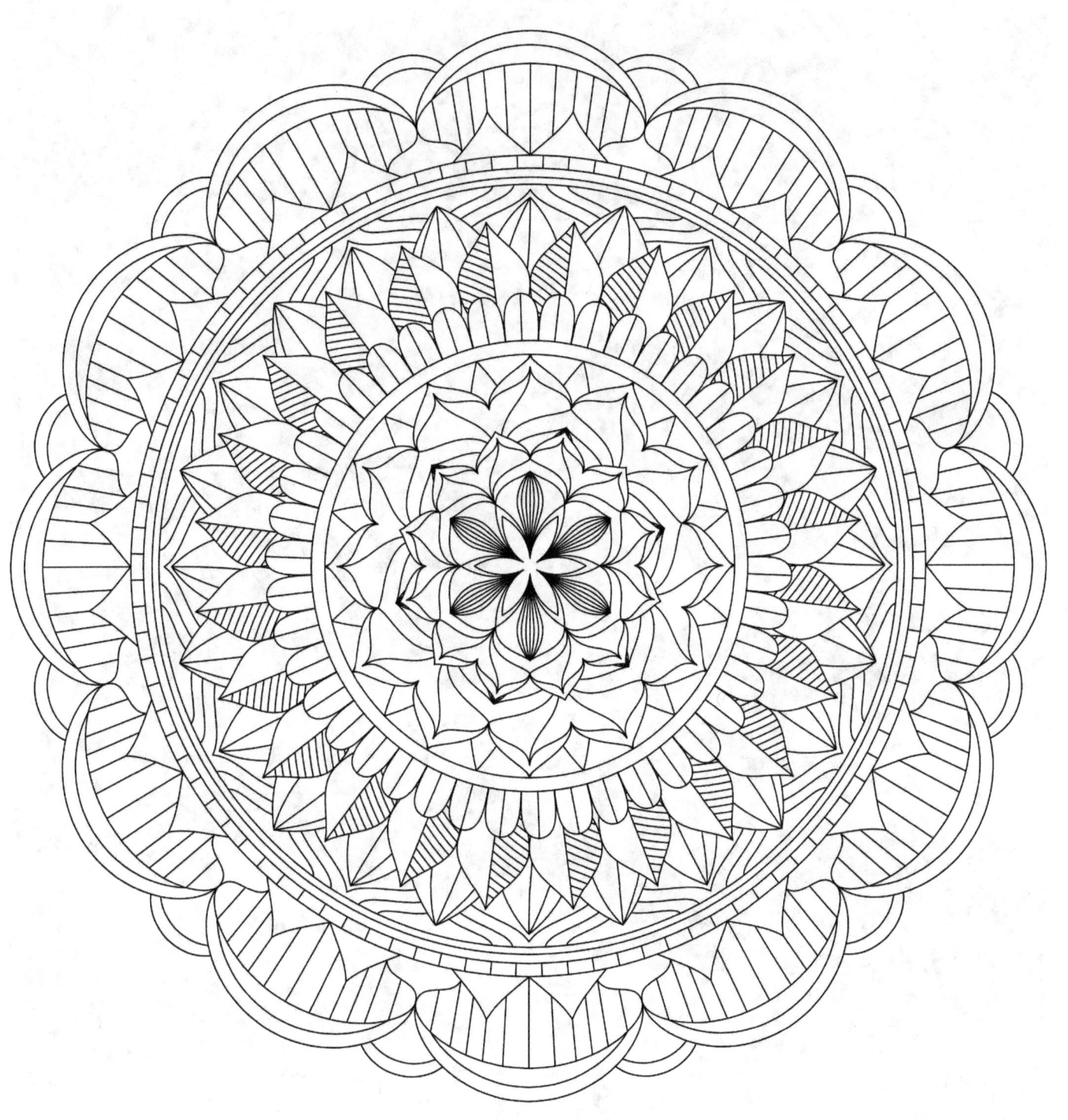

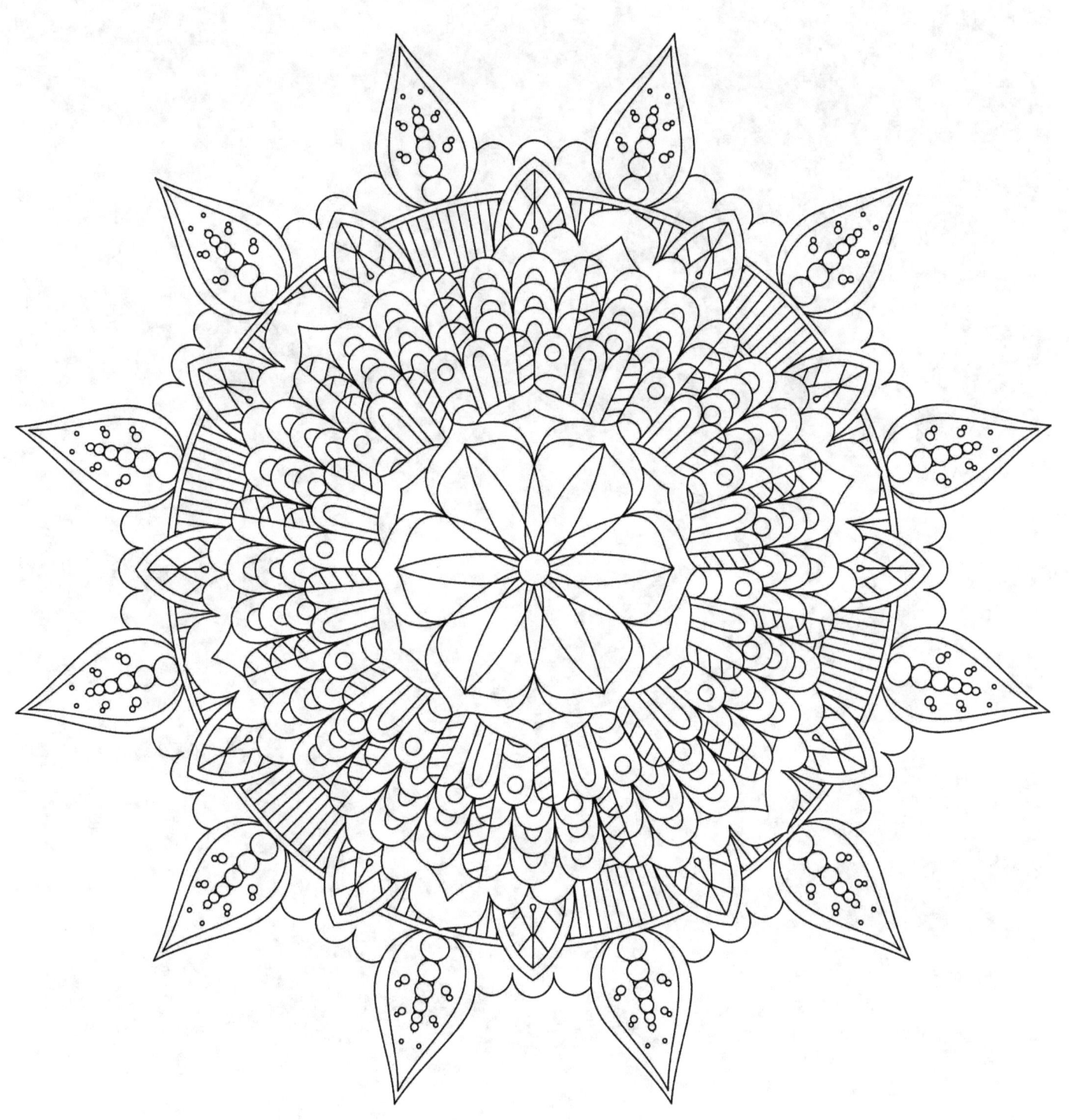

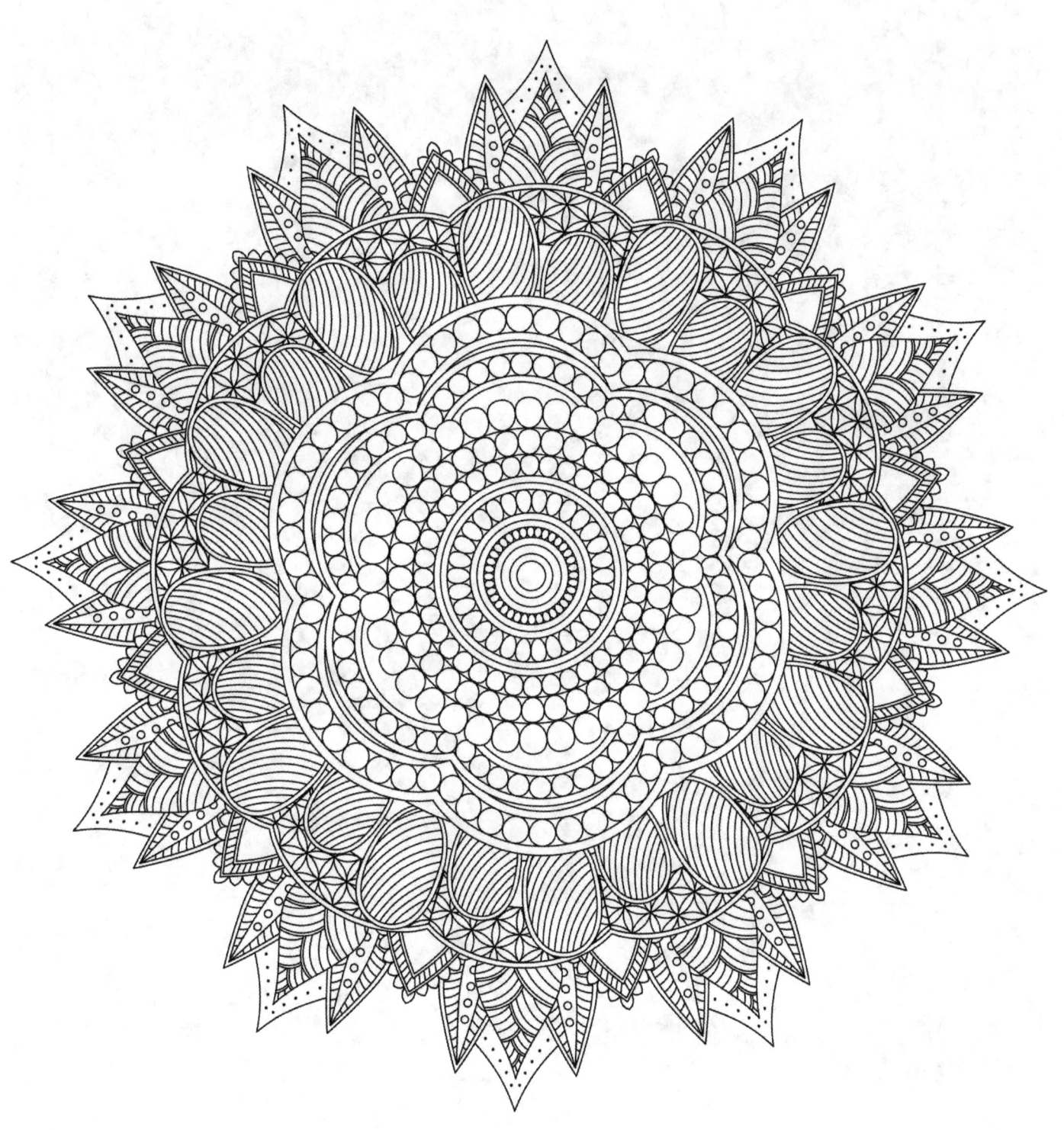

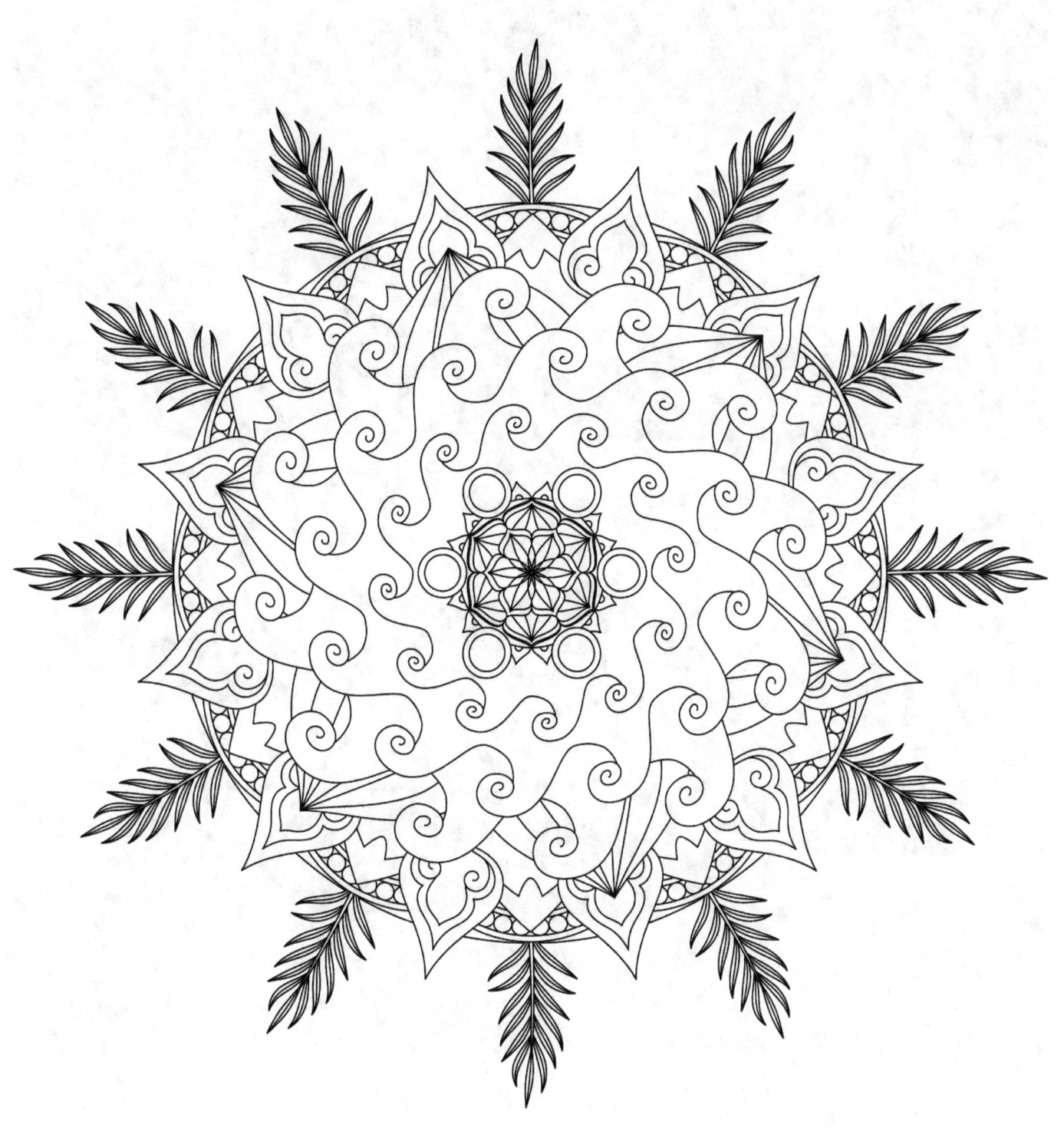

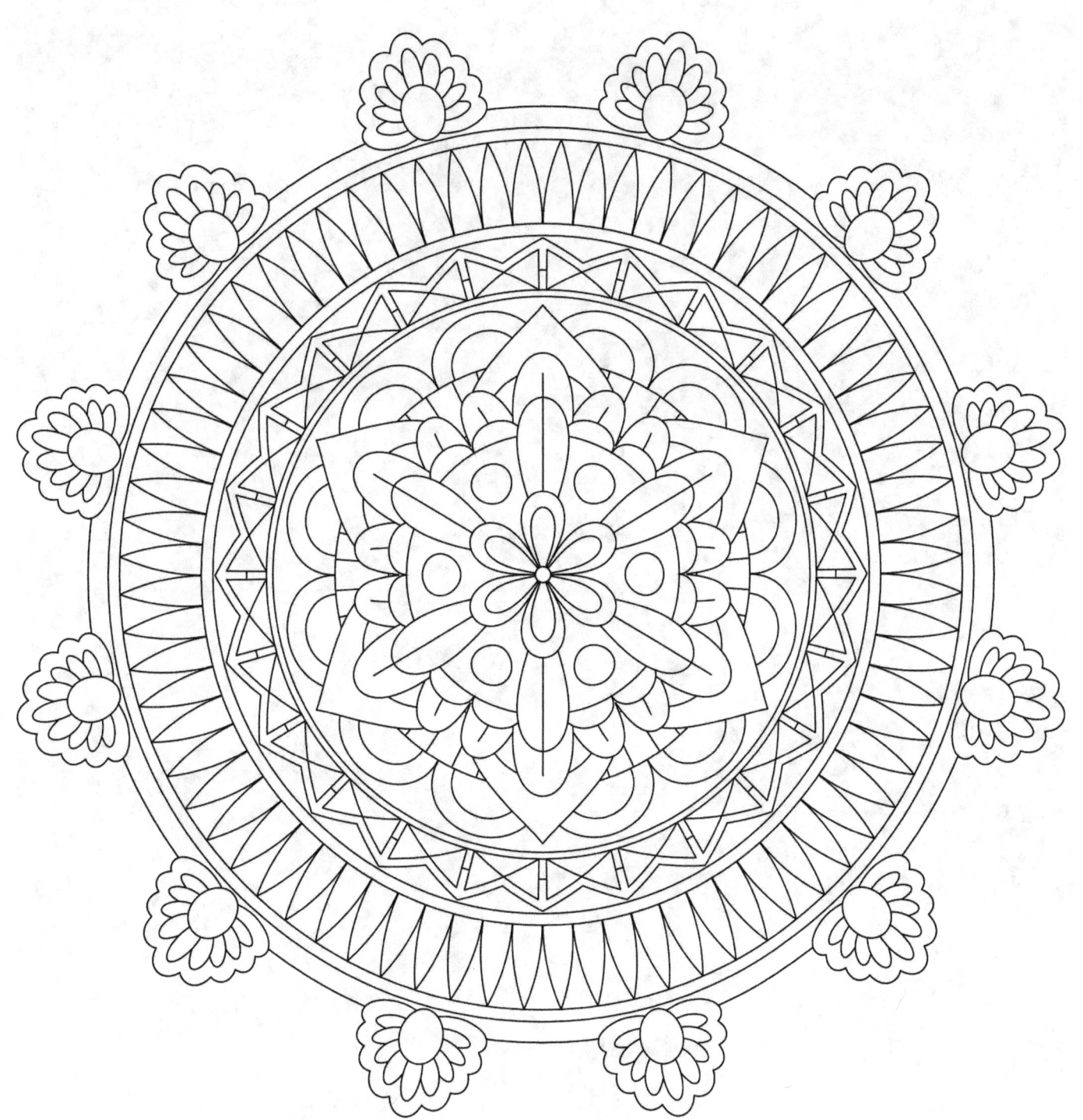

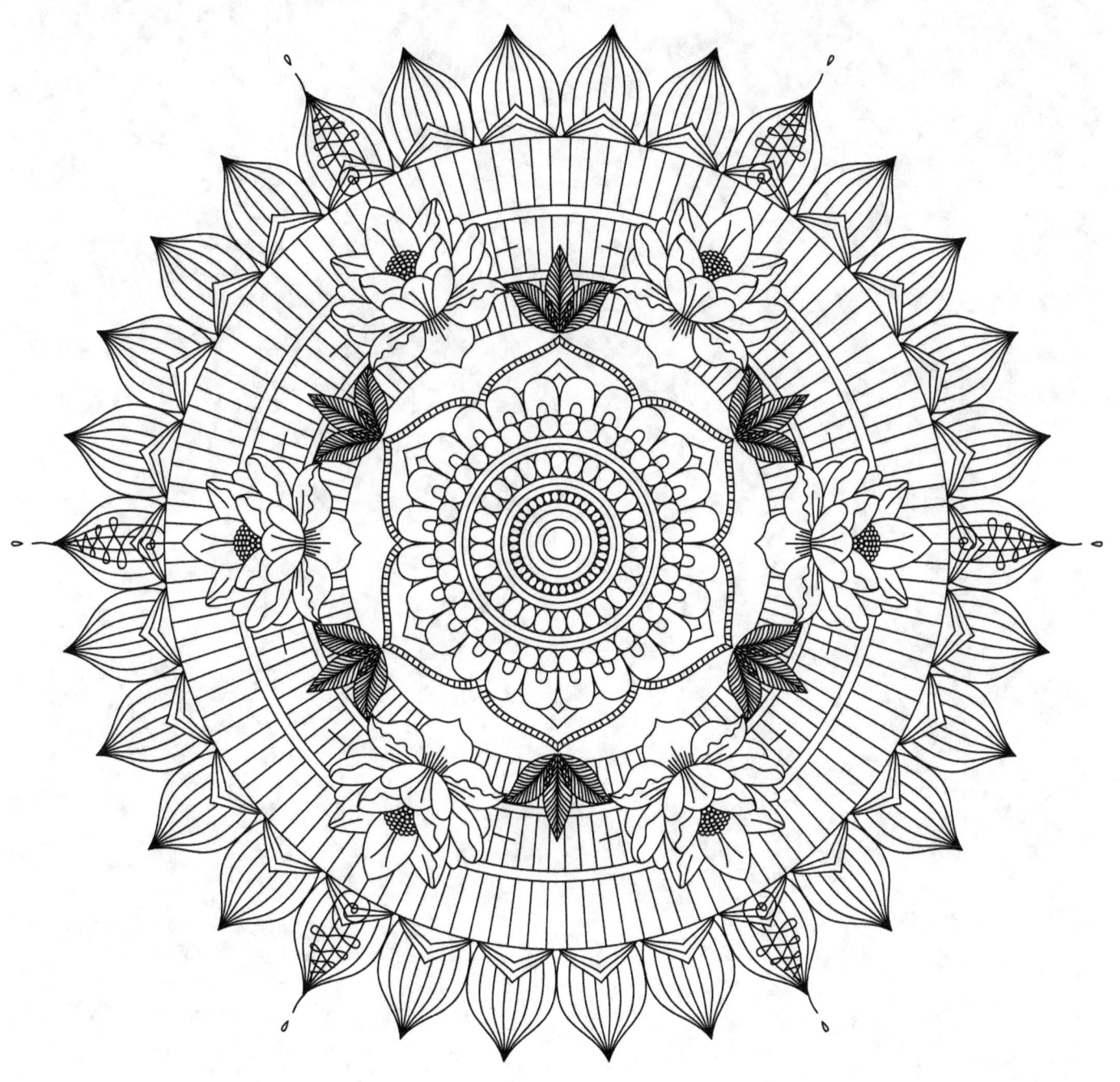

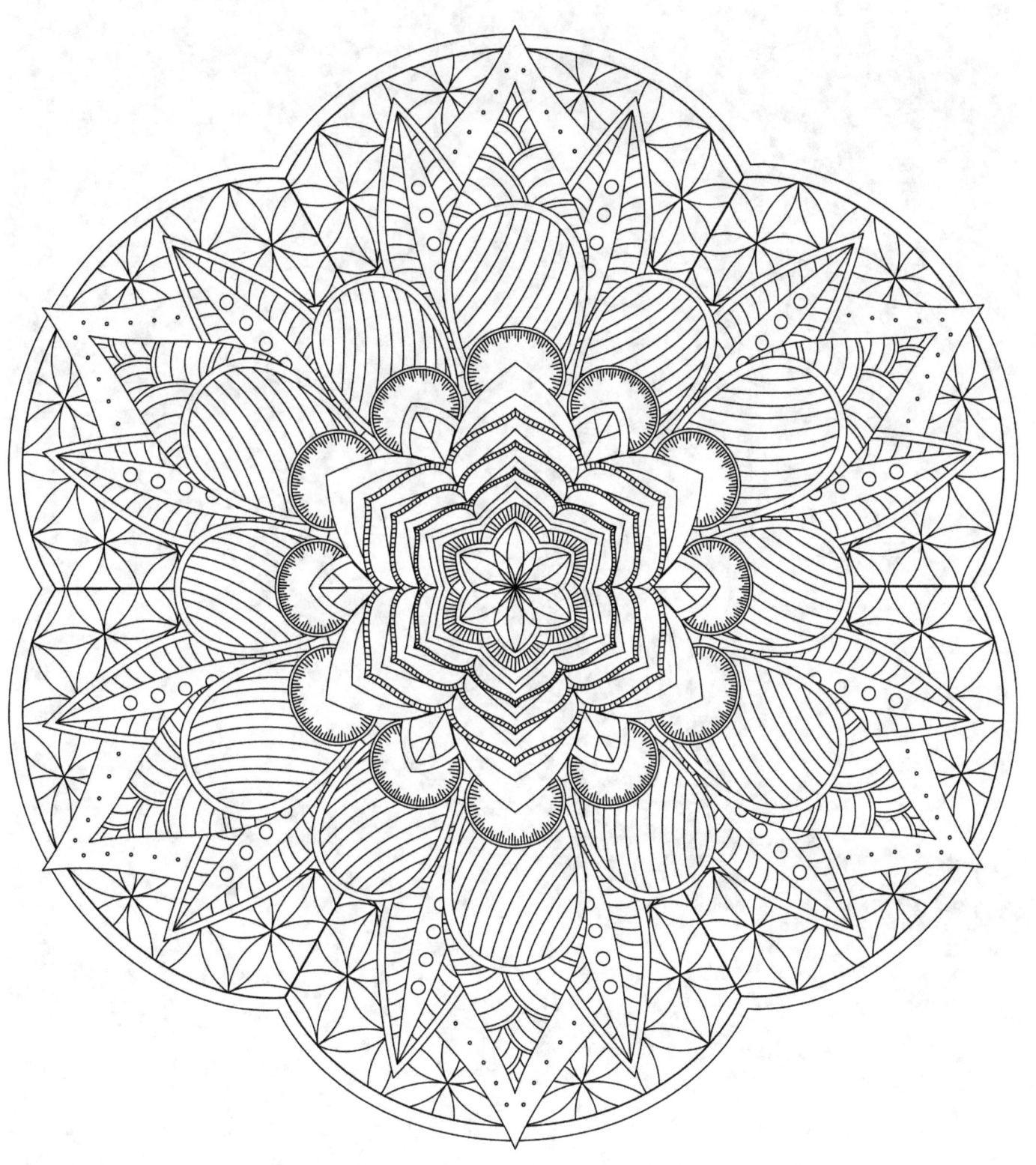

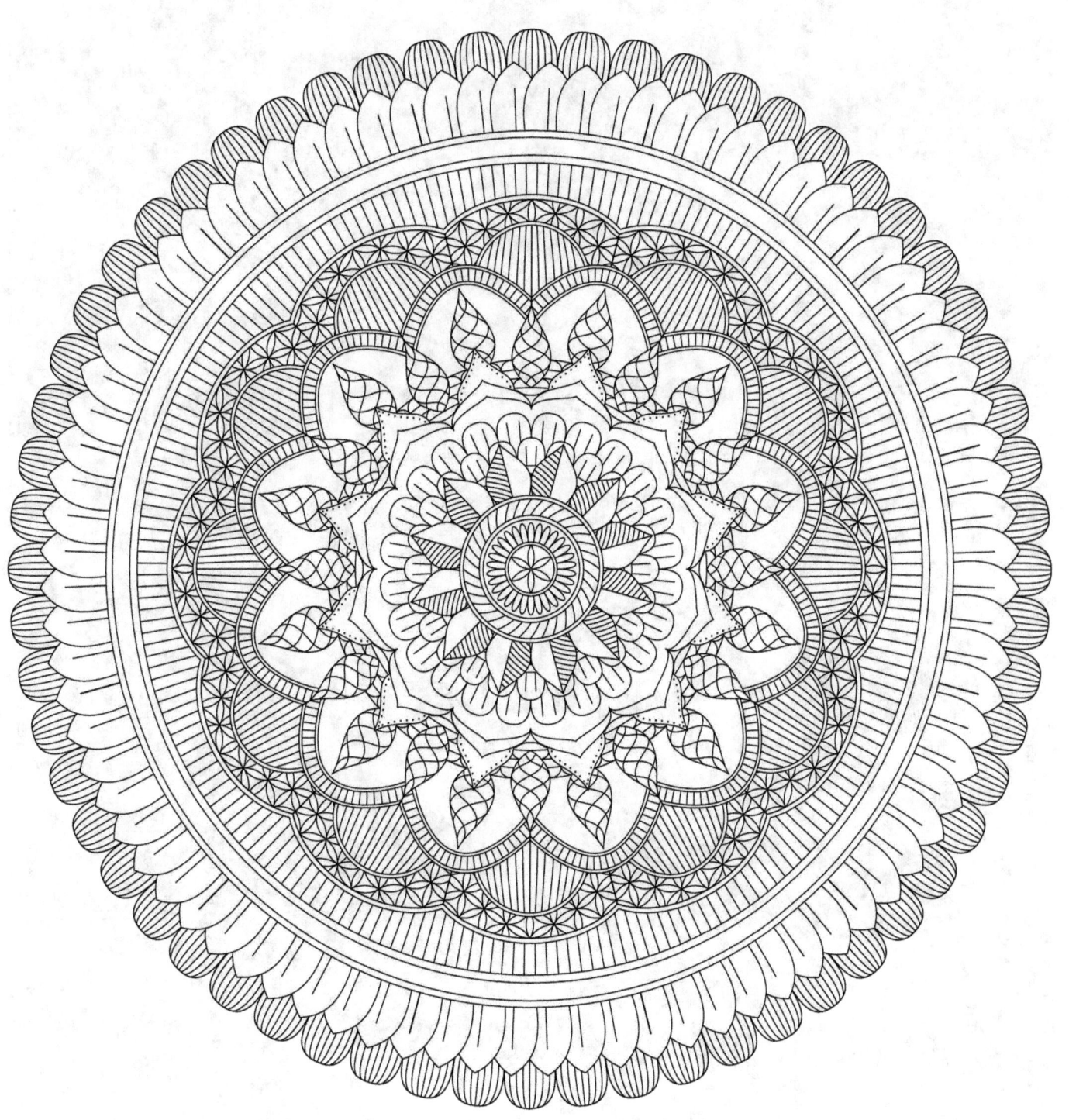

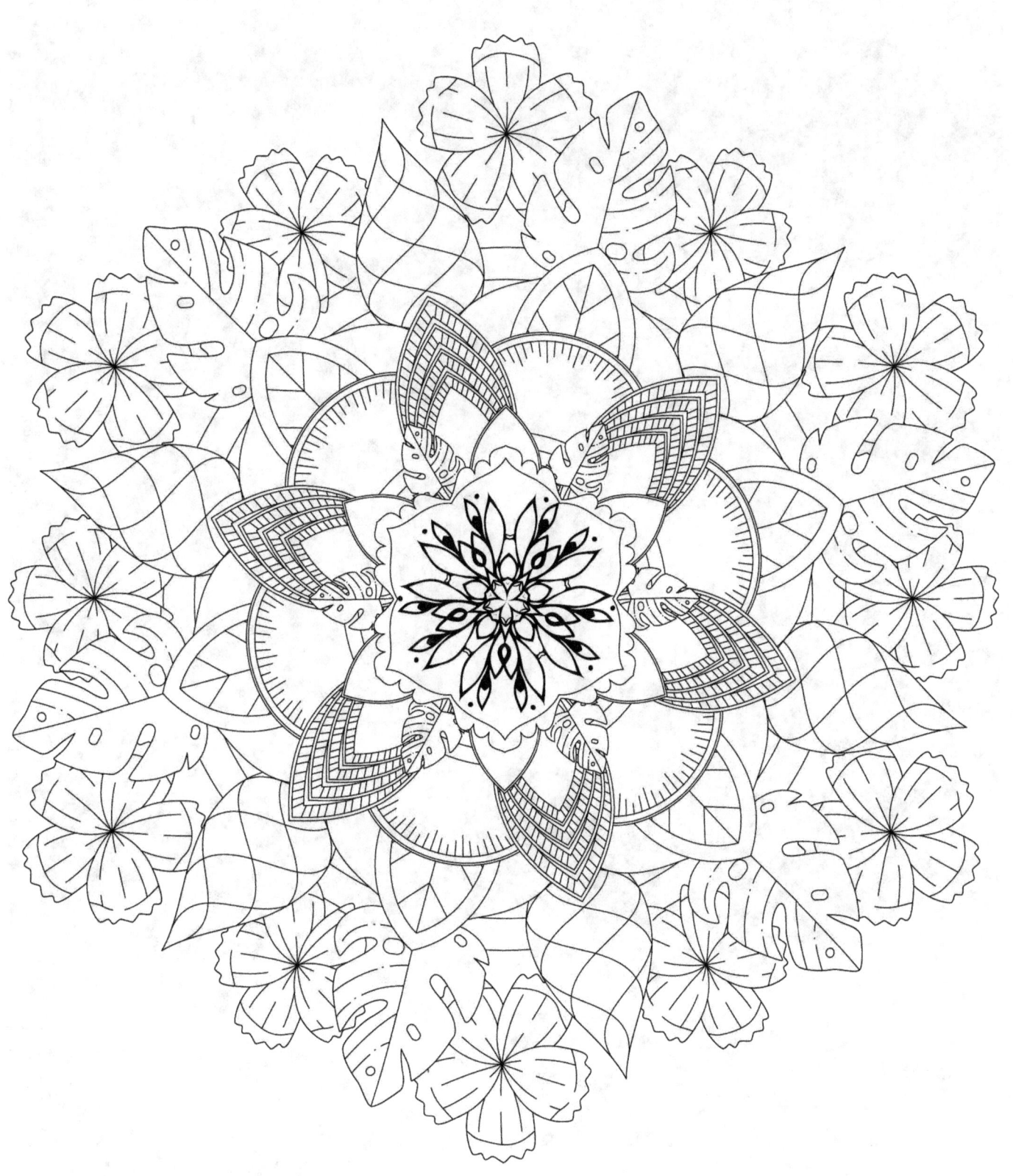

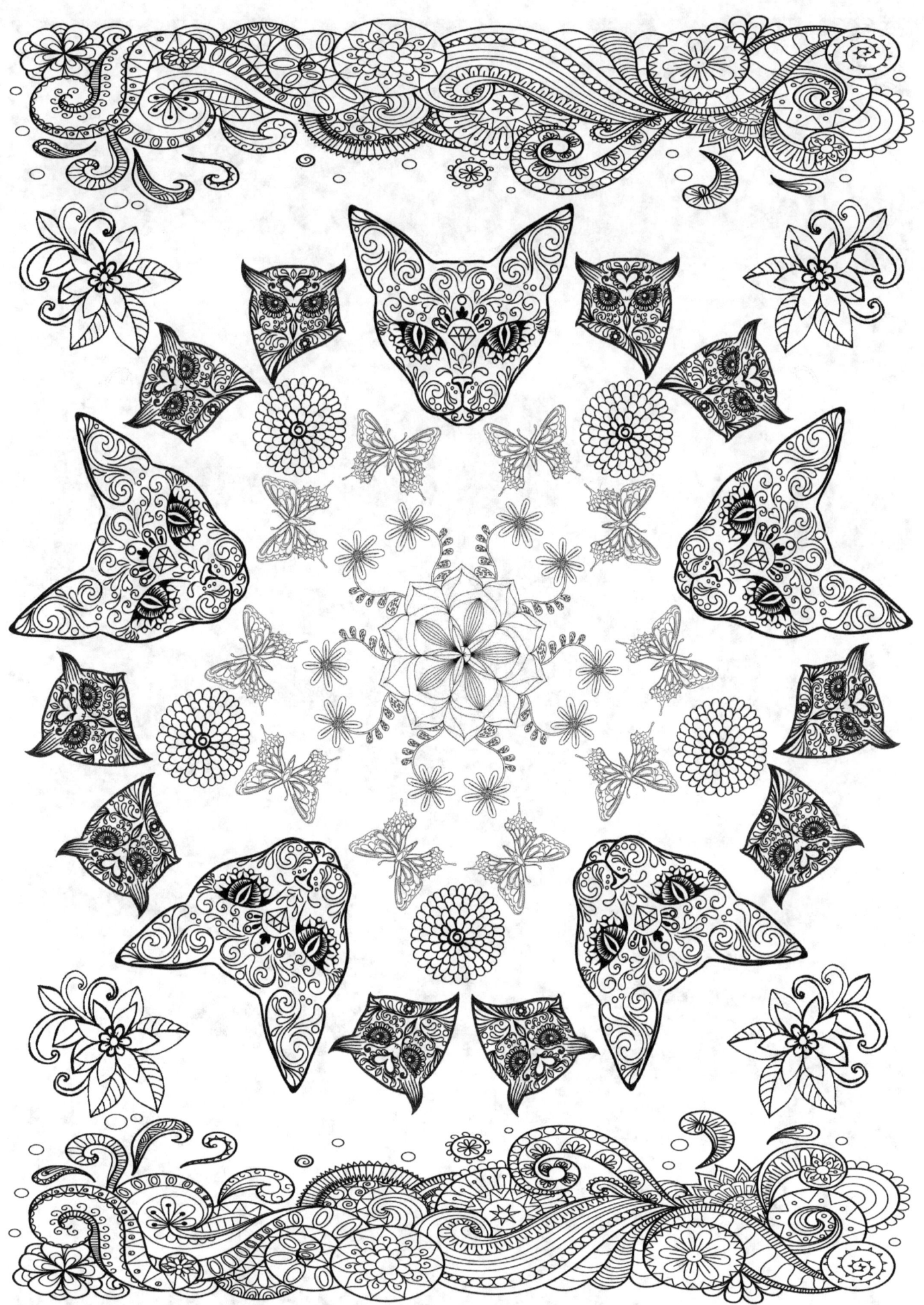

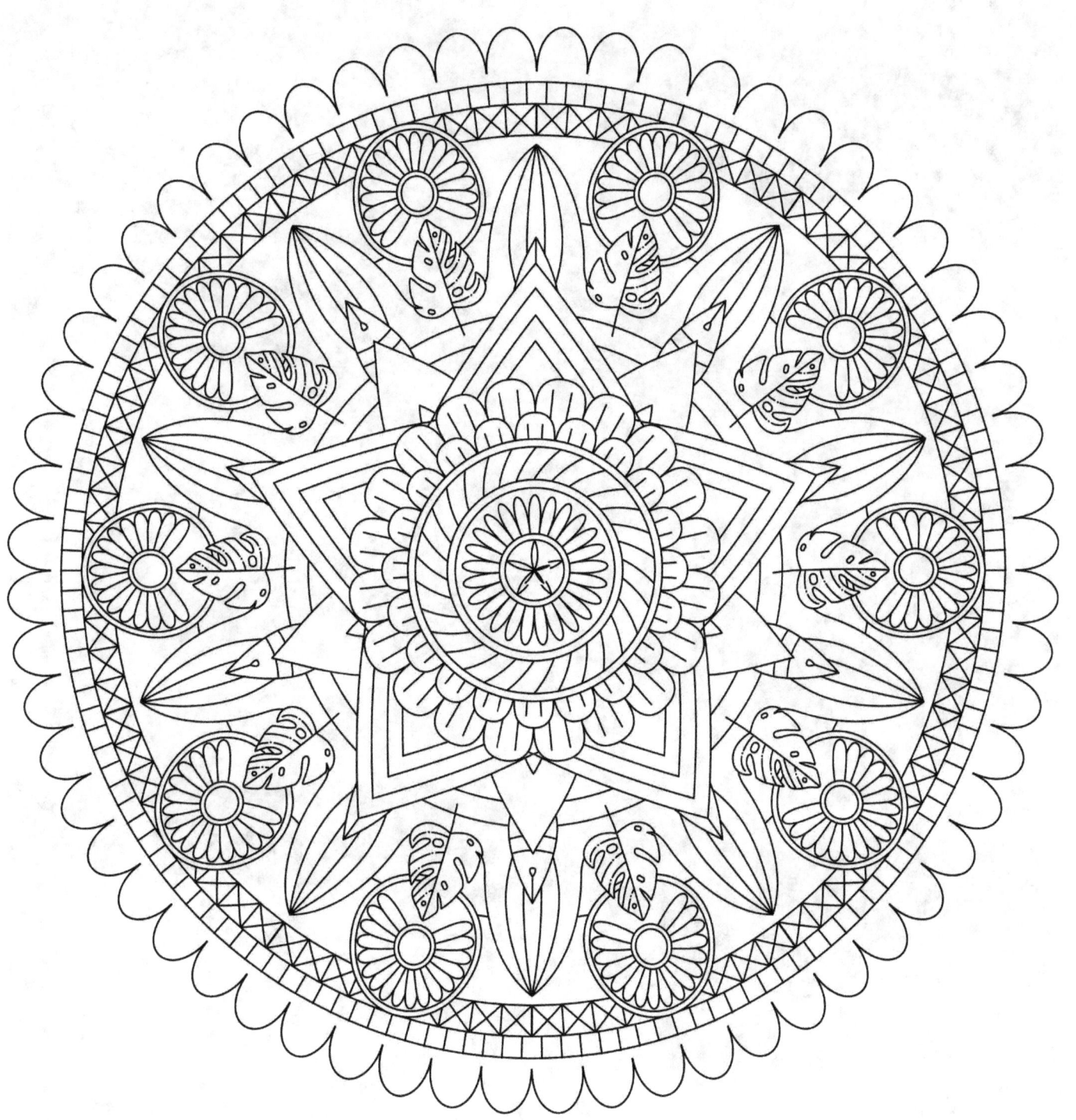

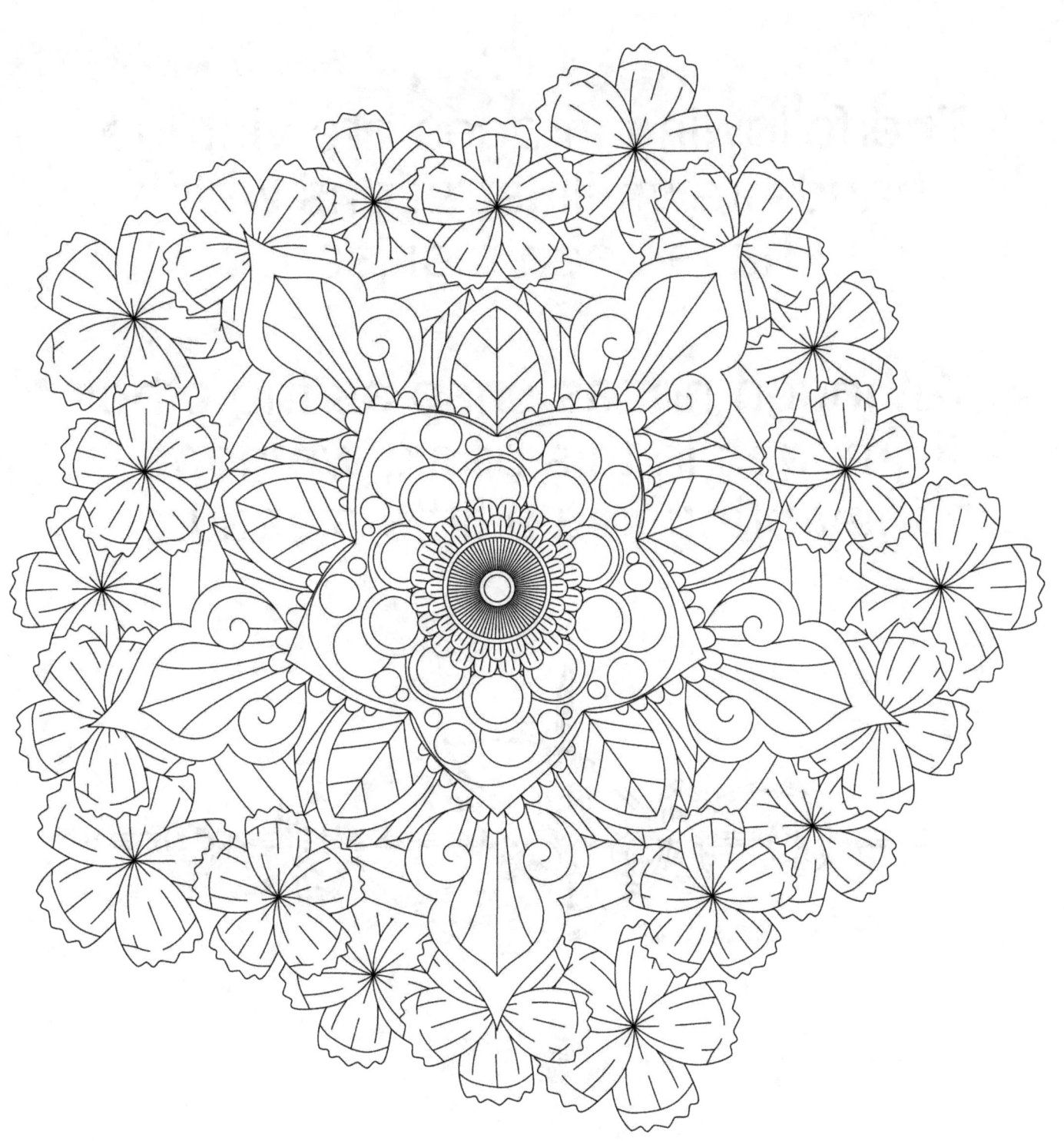

Bonus Section!

The following images are vintage, hand-drawn illustrations which have been digitised.

Although not as crisp as the other images in this book, we hope they bring you a little pleasure.

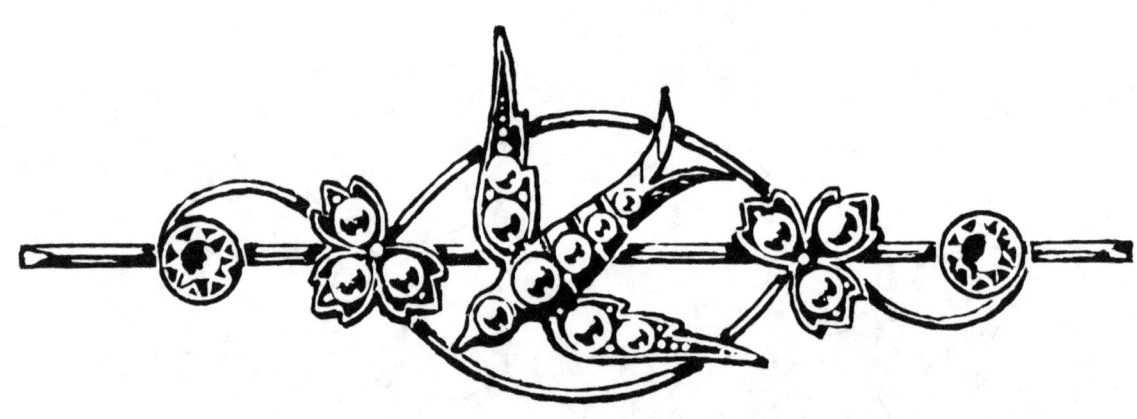

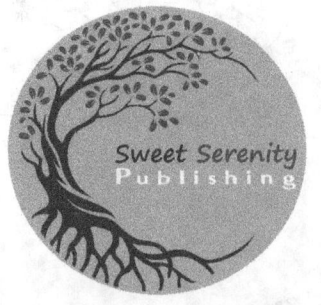

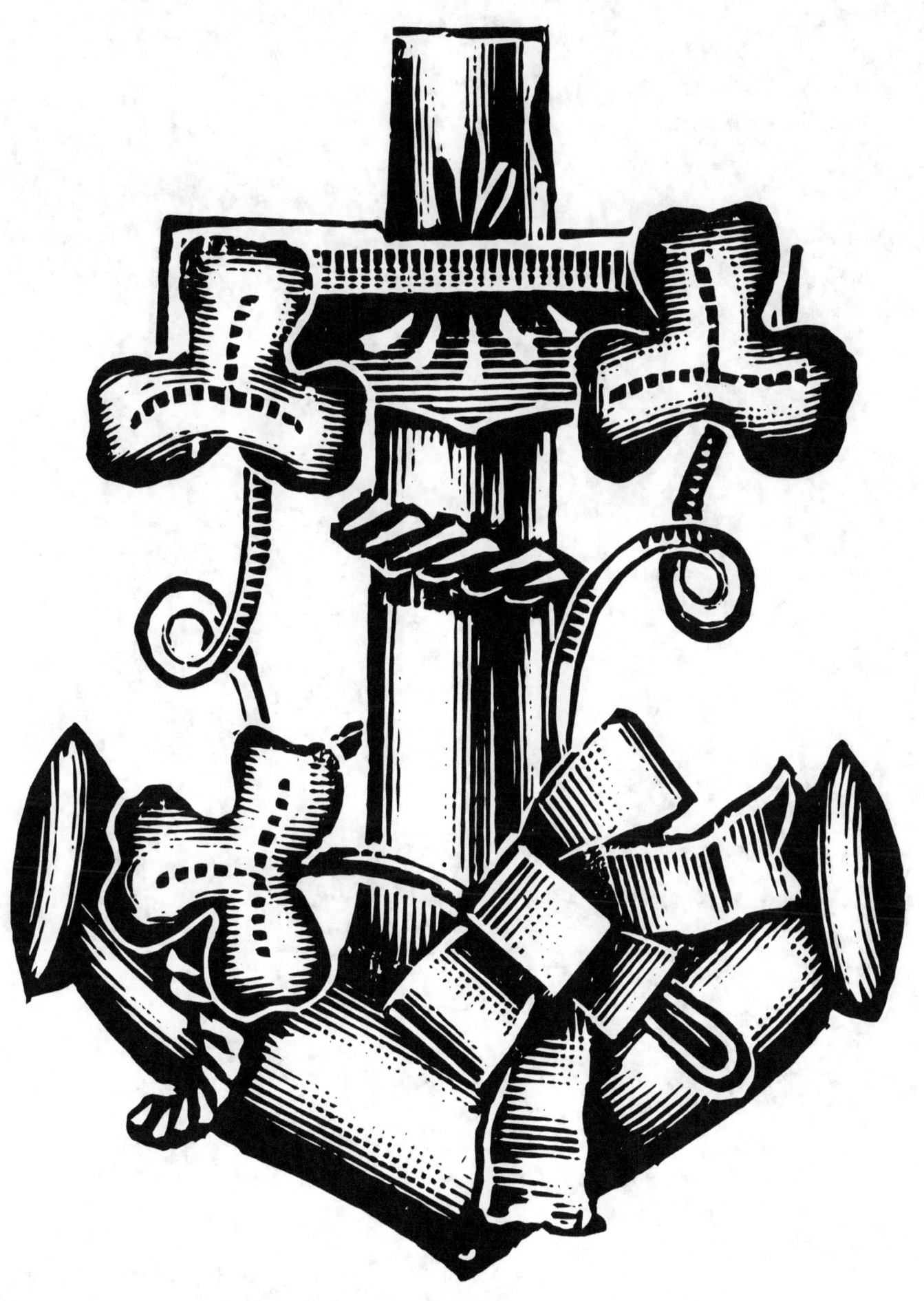

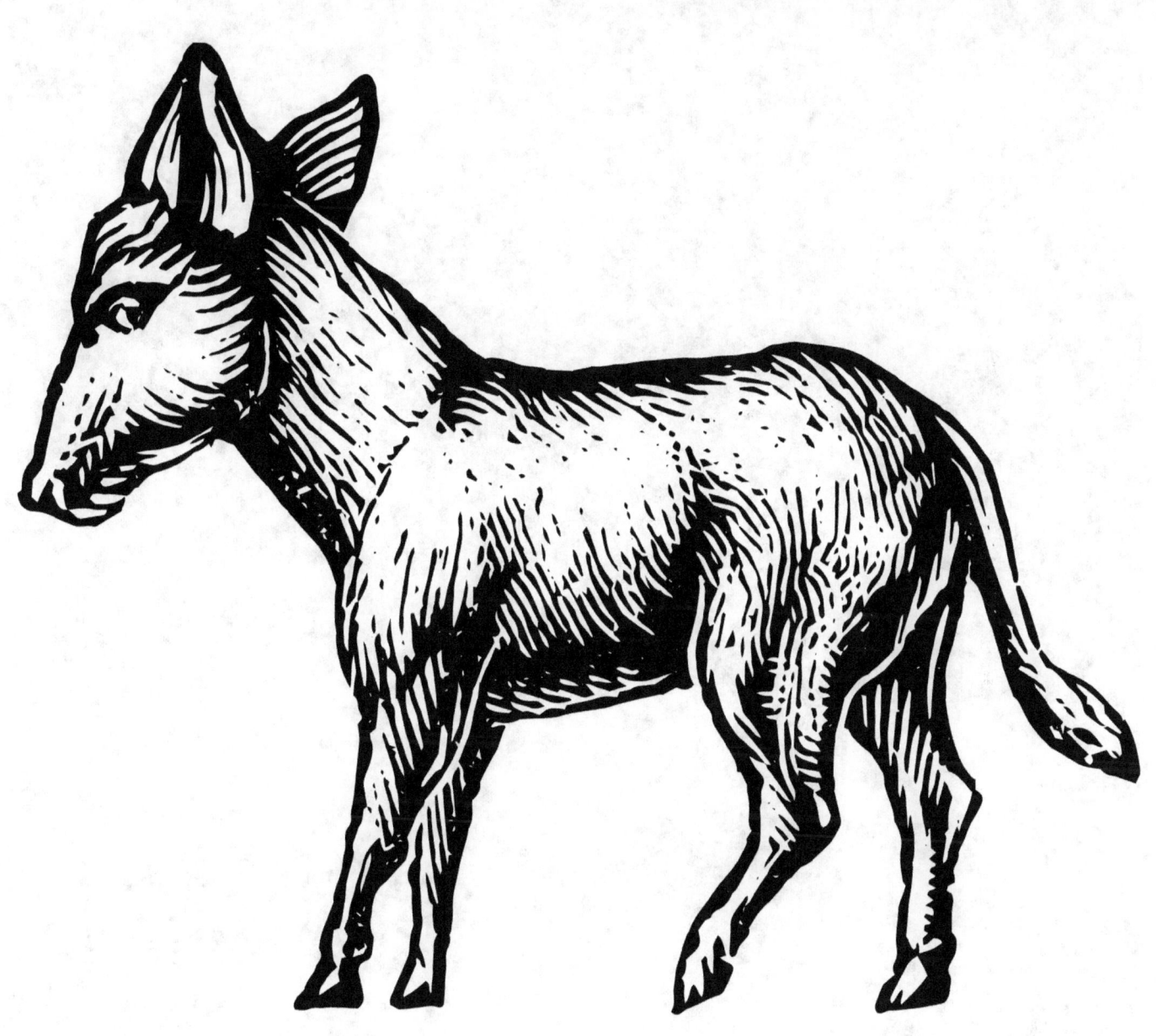

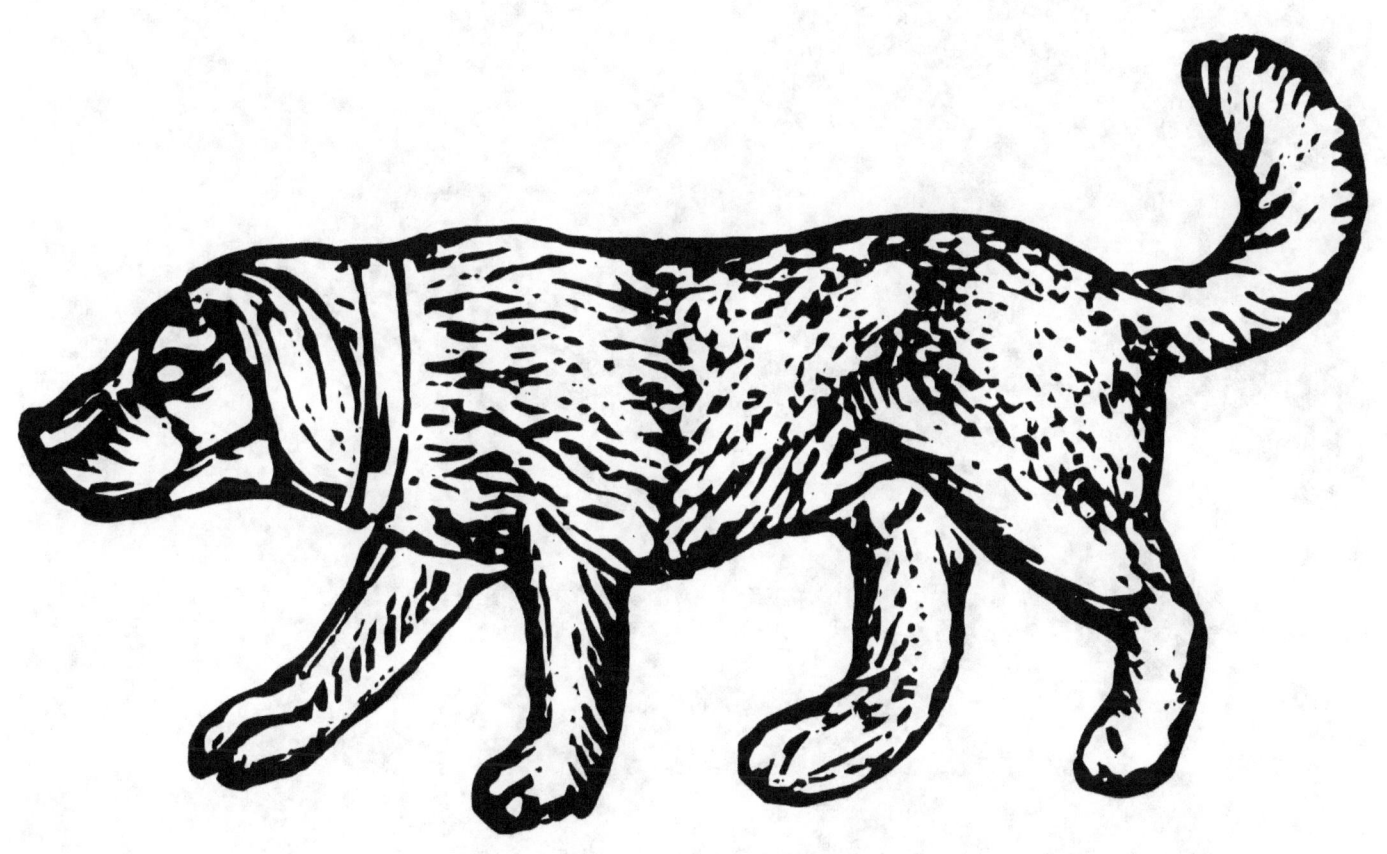

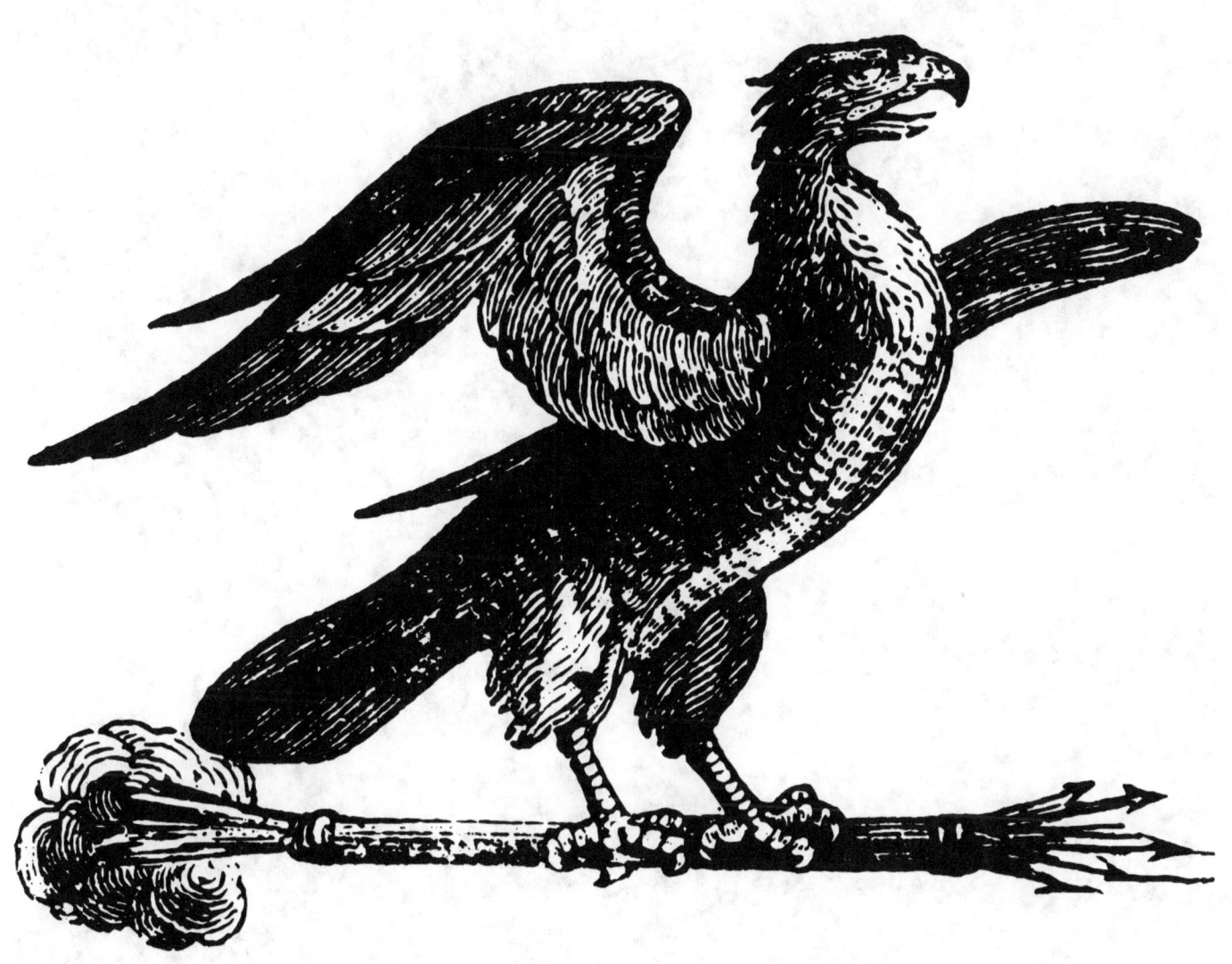

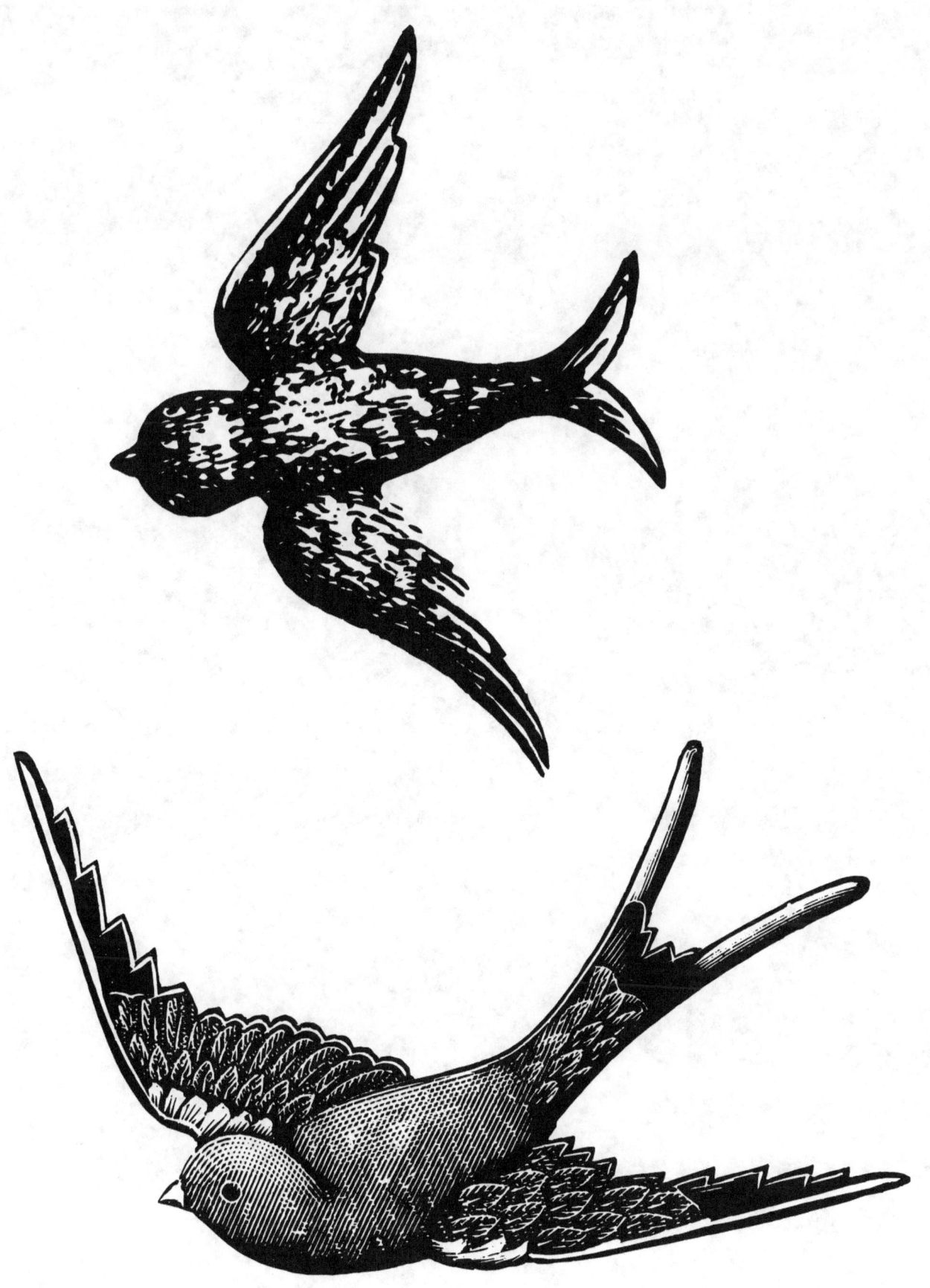

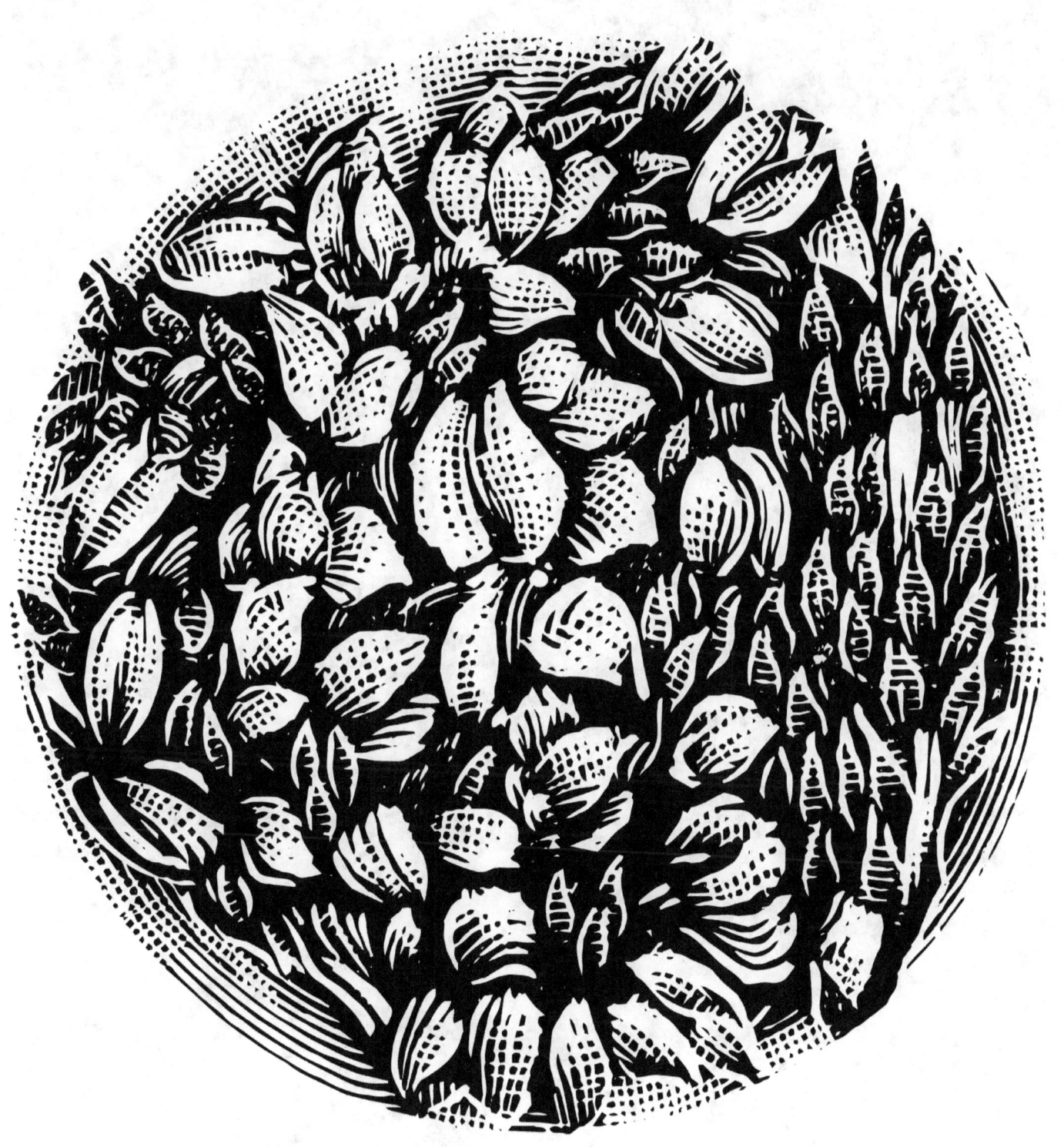

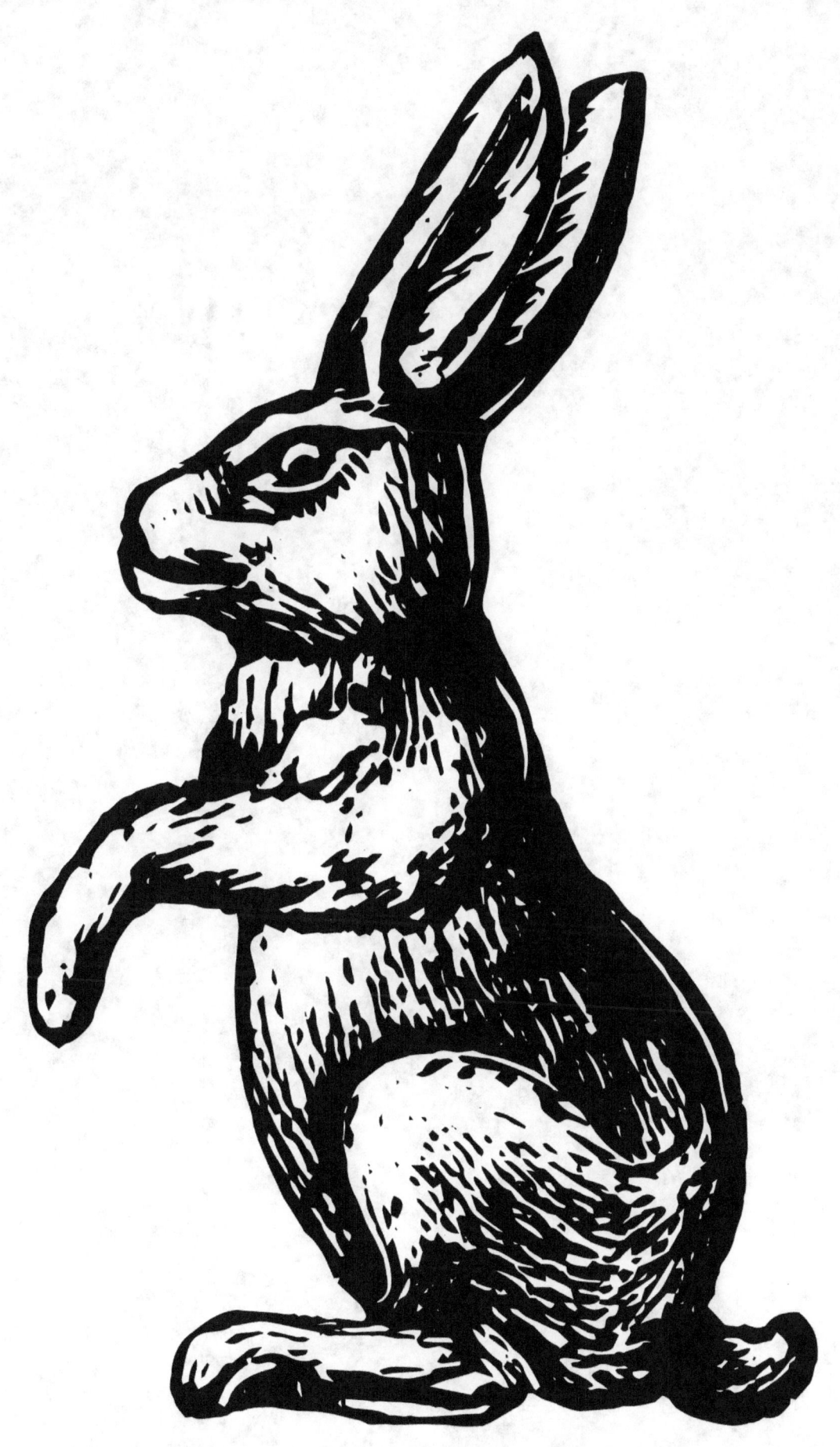

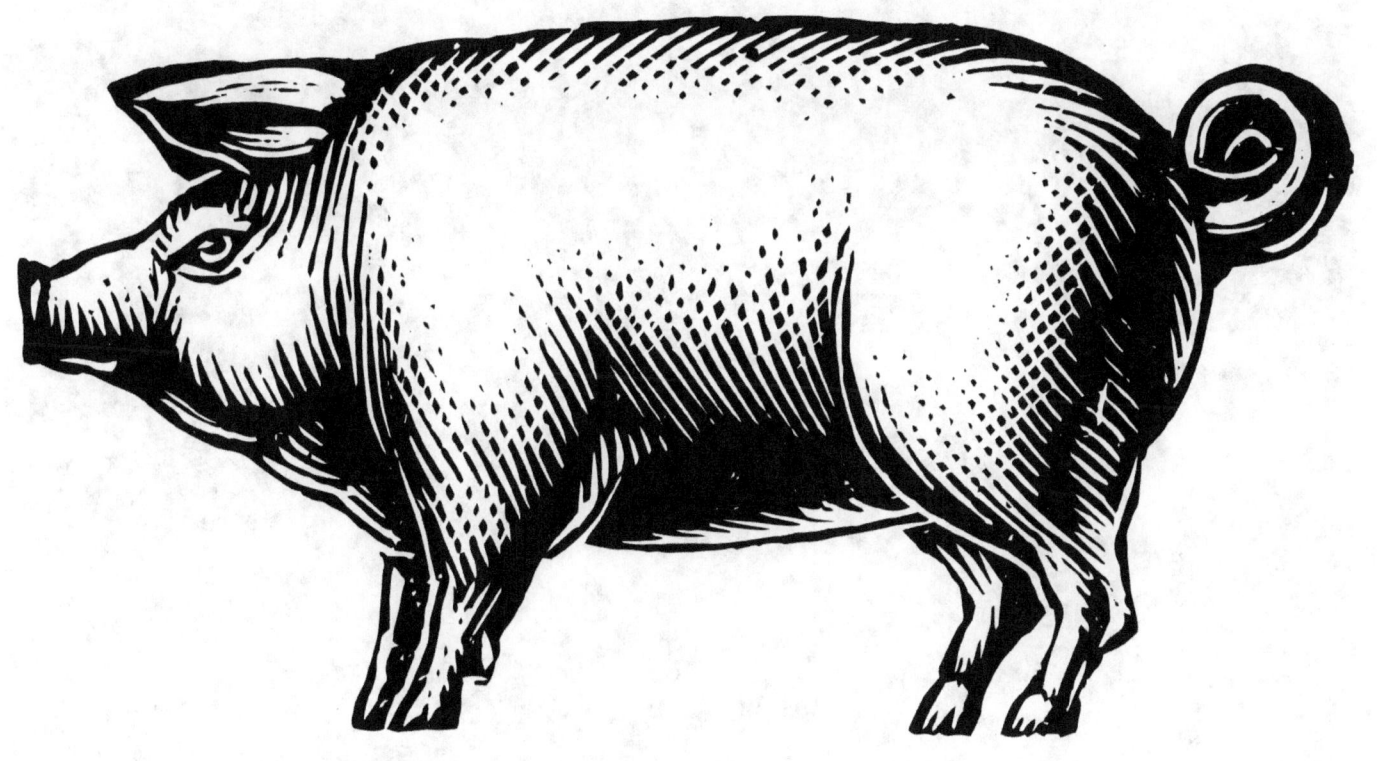
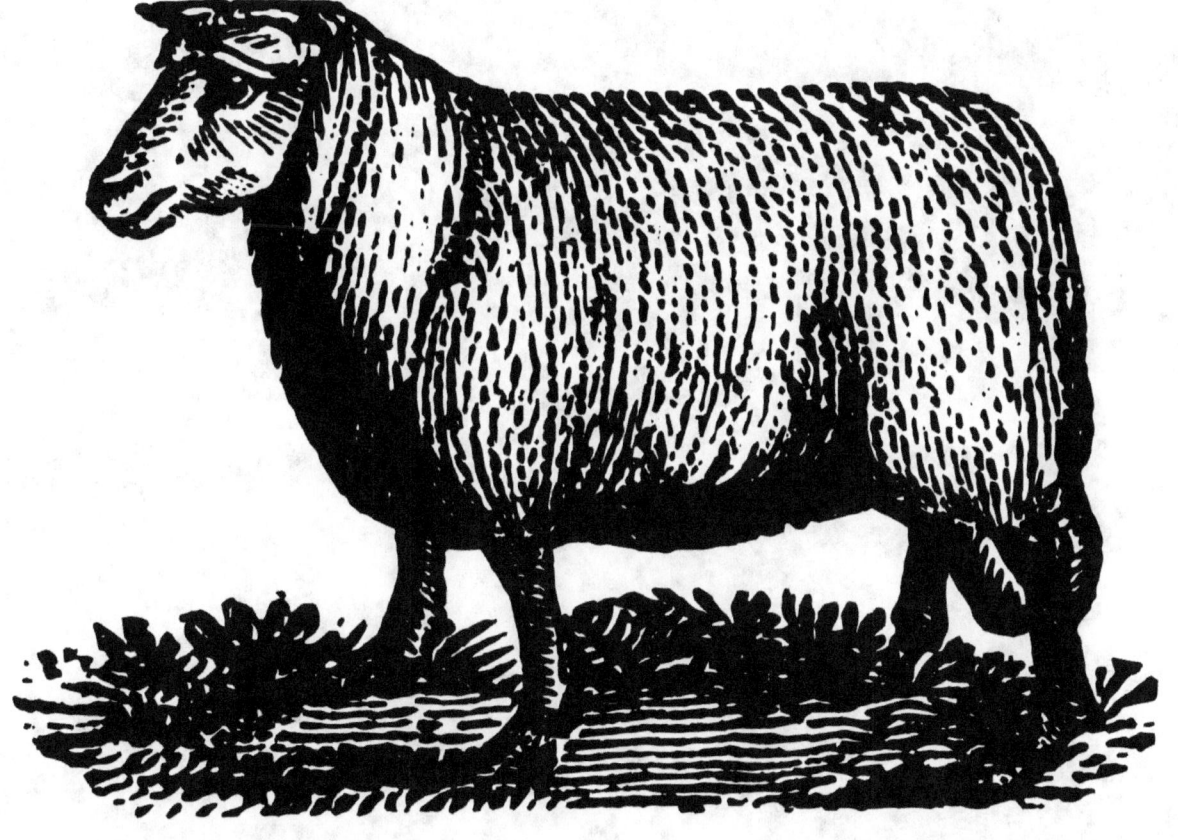

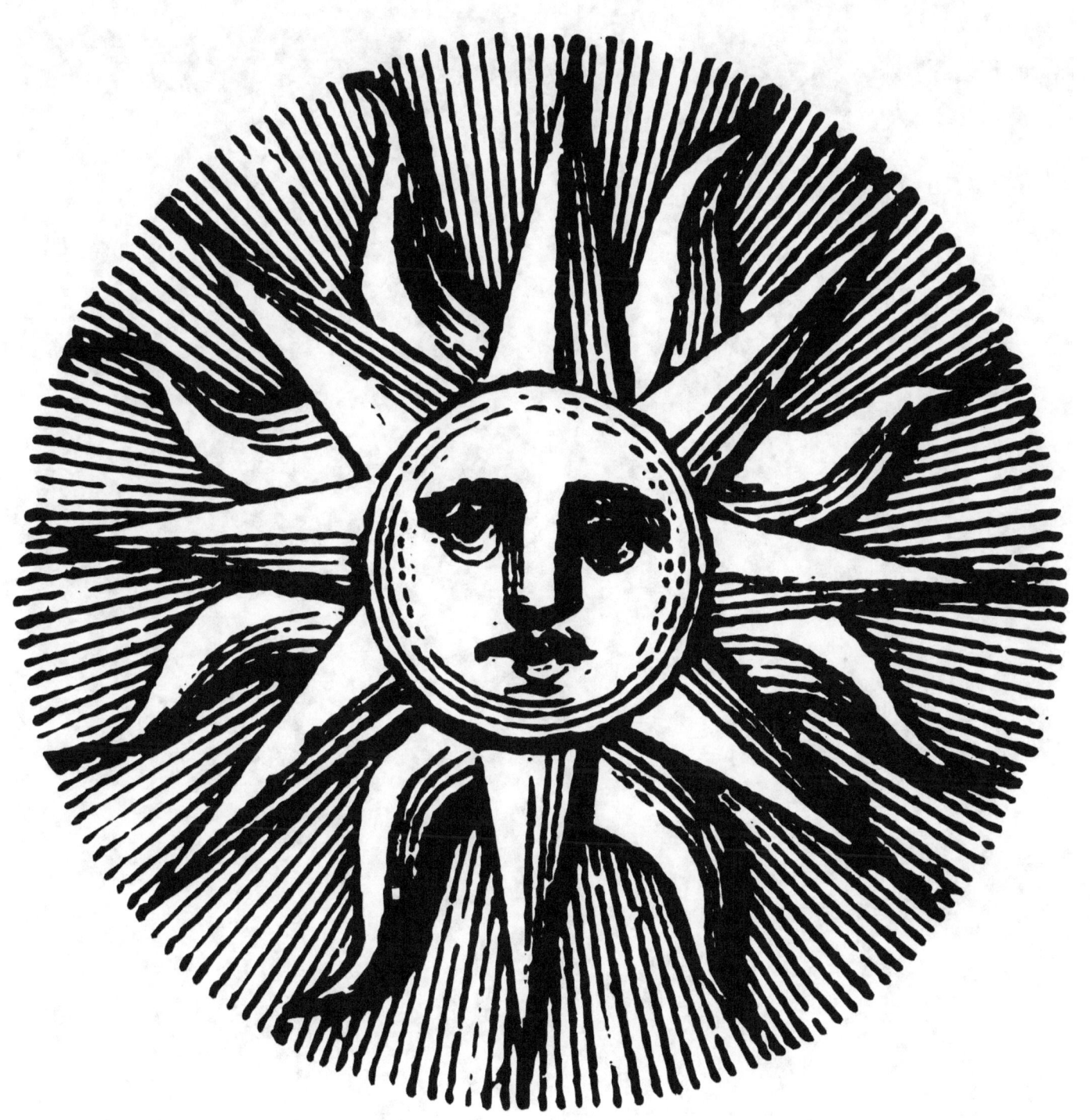

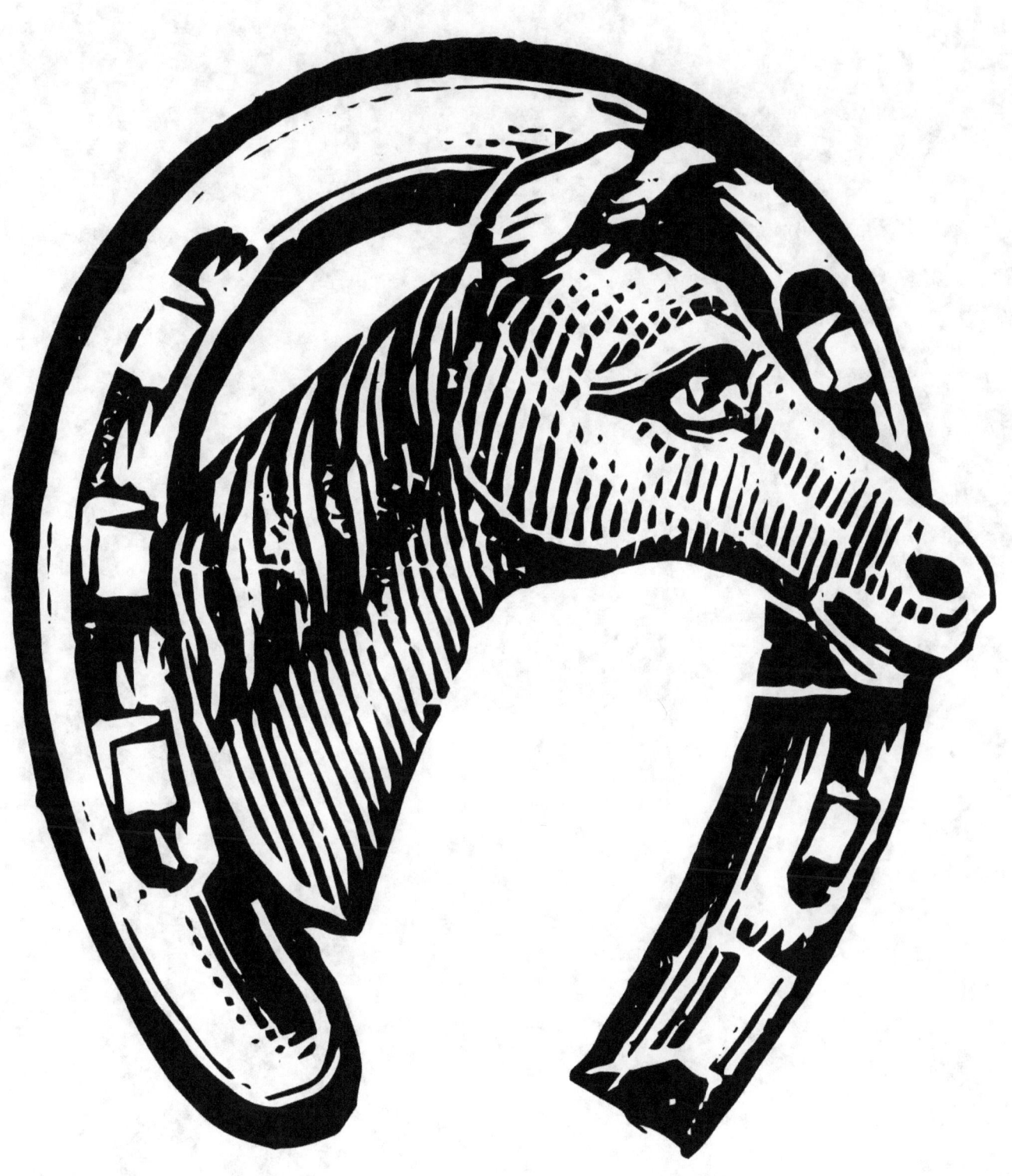

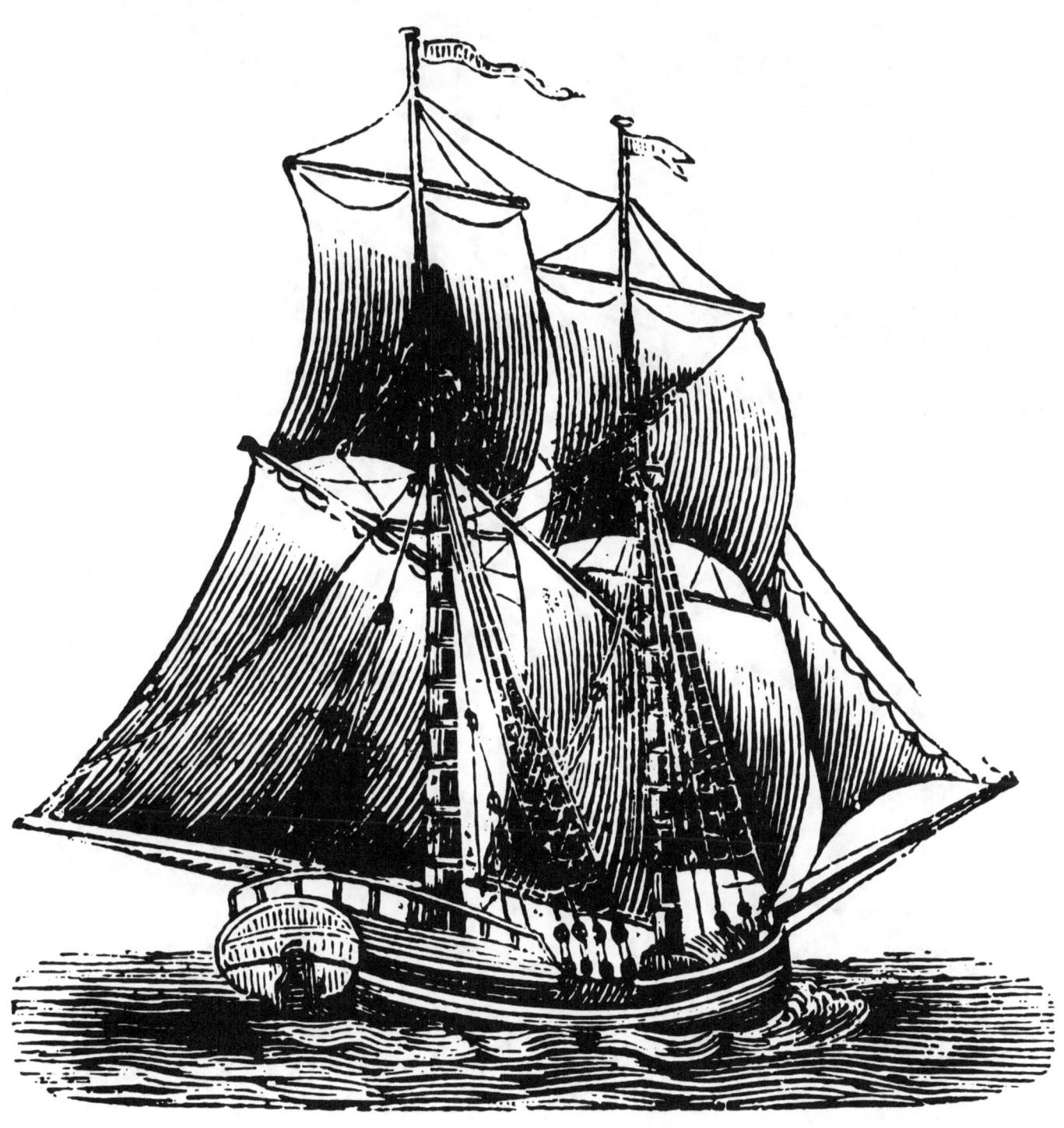

www.ingramcontent.com/pod-product-compliance
Lightning Source LLC
Chambersburg PA
CBHW060415220526
45465CB00008B/2895